Narcissa

with b̶...

regards

Doris Arrington

3/71

L'ABRI

L'ABRI

EDITH SCHAEFFER

Illustrated by Deirdre Ducker

TYNDALE HOUSE PUBLISHERS
Wheaton, Illinois

Distributed in Canada by
Home Evangel Books Ltd.
Toronto, Ontario

I dedicate this book to my husband, Fran, and to Priscilla, Susan, Deborah and Franky . . . without whom there would have been no story to tell.

SBN 854 79371 2

The map of *L'Abri*, Huémoz, was drawn by the author. The illustrations of the "L'Abri Day of Prayer", and "Les Mélèzes Helpers" lists were also drawn by the author, and originally posted up at Chalet les Mélèzes.

This Tyndale House edition published by arrangement with The Norfolk Press and Henry E. Walter Ltd. Printed in U.S.A.

Foreword

THIS BOOK and my books form a unity.

The work of *L'Abri* has two inter-related aspects. First, there is the attempt to give an honest answer to honest questions—intellectually and upon a careful exegetical base. My books, *The God Who is There*, *Escape from Reason* and *Death in the City* are directed to this aspect.

The second aspect is the demonstration that the Personal-Infinite God is *really there* in our generation. When twentieth-century people come to *L'Abri* they are faced with these two aspects simultaneously, as the two sides of a single coin. Now, in this book, this second side is presented.

Switzerland   FRANCIS A. SCHAEFFER

Acknowledgements

THE mention of people—some by name, others with only initials—has been important in giving the story covered in this book accuracy. The author wishes to thank those whose stories have entered into the warp and woof of the fabric woven through the past twenty years. Also, it is important not only to say that this book is a condensation of all that happened, and that only a portion of the detail of any one story has been given, but also to say that many, many people who have had an important place in the life of *L'Abri* through the past years have not been mentioned at all, because of the lack of space. It would have taken a whole series of books to tell the stories of people who have come to *L'Abri*, and to tell all the thrilling stories of people involved in praying, or in the answers to prayer which have taken place. A whole book could be written concerning the romances, weddings, and new homes which have sprung up from *L'Abri*, for instance. Hence, if anyone is disappointed because of being "left out" please remember that some pages have had to be "cut" and "edited". Other chapters have never been written because of the lack of space! So, with the acknowledgement to those who have added to the story by "walking through" some of the pages, I would thank others for having added to the reality of all that has happened through the years because of their "walking through" the actual history in one way and another.

And I couldn't have written this book without saying how much Switzerland as a country has meant to us and especially thanking the people in the Commune of Ollon and the village of Huémoz, who have allowed us to make our home here.

Contents

Chalet les Mélèzes, Huémoz

Introduction

CLINGING TO the side of a steep alp the warm wood tones of a new chalet glow in the brilliant sunshine of a golden October day. Its one big room is flooded with this same sun streaming through the huge picture windows which frame the view of the Rhône valley, and the silver streak of the Rhône itself winding through it. The peaks of the Dents du Midi cannot long hold one's eye as the sparkling diamond white of the glacier demands attention. Peak after peak together form a panorama that is breathtaking, yet the green of the woods and the changing colours of the rocks draw one's glance to details and away from the total sweep of the view. The room itself is recognisable as a chapel, with its pulpit and orderly rows of chairs, and the jewel of a Flentrop organ in one corner blending its mahogany and burnished copper pipes with the pine walls and arched ceiling of the room. A huge stone fireplace at one side speaks of other uses for the room than just formal services.

This chapel, standing on ground that such a short time ago was just steep stubbly grass, rocks, a few trees and beehives, was built with the brocade and velvet costumes of an opera singer! At least a portion of the chapel had these costumes as the "source material" exchanged for wood and stone. Its existence, and the existence of the room below—filled with twenty-three desks, each with its own set of earphones and tape recorders—is a miracle. Near the chapel are a number of chalets which have a special relationship to it. There is Chalet les Mélèzes, which seems to be overflowing with people as strains of Beethoven float out of one of the windows, and voices buzz in serious discussion as people are clustered in groups sitting on benches or on long, hand hewn tables of oak, or under an apple tree on the grass, or near open windows of the long living-room. A voice drones on as another group sit around a tape-recorder in the sun room of Chalet Beau Site, just beyond the garden next to Les Mélèzes.

Across the road float the golden tones of a magnificent soprano voice practising, and if you come closer the tap of a journalist's typewriter can be heard as background accompaniment. This is Chalet le Chesalet.

On the other side of Chalet les Mélèzes the garden is full of wheel-chairs, and little groups of cerebral palsy patients play a game of ball or swing on swings. Bellevue's long sweep of roof, sloping almost to the ground, covers a marvellous rehabilitation home for cerebral palsy children—and is there because of what took place in Chalet les Mélèzes some years ago.

Some distance down the back dirt road the laughing voices of small children come up from a garden, and the voices of girls chattering in the sun as they peel potatoes harmonise with the children's voices. This is Chalet Tzi No, and it also has much in common with the other chalets.

Nearby Chalet Argentine's wide balcony holds the easel of an artist at work, and the typewriter table of one who is busily copying a manuscript. Down a steep dirt road, a sharp turn to the right and up another dirt road one is brought to Bethany, with bedrooms filled with double-decker beds. It, too, is a part of this whole complex, as are a chalet belonging to a violinist, some rented rooms in the village, and occasionally other rented chalets, also a field surrounded by a tree hedge, and a chalet which announces it is "for sale" are now, or are about to be, involved too.

Is there any name for this place, made up of these various properties? *L'Abri* covers it all—that is, all except that which must come under the heading of the "community": the cerebral palsy home, the violinist and the journalist, and some who rent chalets nearby. *L'Abri* and this community are in a tiny Alpine village at the side of a road leading to a well-known ski resort, so tucked away from today's world that to live there seems, in a sense, to be buried.

What does L'Abri mean?

The word is simply French for "shelter". *L'Abri* is a spiritual shelter for any in need of spiritual help—especially those seeking the answers to the basic philosophical problems with which all who care about finding a meaning or purpose in life have to struggle.

Who is there?

At *L'Abri* there are students from every kind of discipline—philosophy, science, medicine, art, architecture, theology, music, engineering, aeronautics, etc. There are undergraduates, postgraduates, Ph.D.'s, and those who have been professors, doctors, lawyers, vicars, pastors, engineers, dancers, opera singers, writers, editors, sculptors or violinists. They range in age from the early teens to the sixties. There are Indians, Dutch, English, Scots, Italians, French, South Africans and Rhodesians, Americans, Swiss, New Zealanders, Australians, Japanese, Koreans, and so on. The people are not only an international mixture, but also a mixture in age, and in background and interests.

Why have they come?

They have one main thing in common . . . most of them are truly serious in seeking the answers to the basic questions which bother any thinking person. Although they come from backgrounds and beliefs which can be diametrically opposed, there is the searching, the "seeking" which is in some measure present in each one there. The differences are as widely divergent as could be imagined. There are atheists, agnostics, existentialists, Hindus (or those who have some form of Hindu philosophy or religion), Jews of many types of belief or unbelief, Roman Catholics, Liberal Protestants, Buddhists, and also the products of many shades of twentieth-century thinking all based on a relativism which has no absolutes, and no conviction that such a thing as truth even exists. But for the most part, those who come are unsatisfied, and they come with questions, desiring to listen to answers!

How have they come?

They have come in almost as many ways as there are people there. They have heard of *L'Abri* by word of mouth, mostly. One Japanese heard of *L'Abri* in Chicago, and went back to Tokyo by way of this tiny Alpine village. Another bumped into a girl, quite literally, in a taxi in Cairo . . . a girl who had become a Christian in *L'Abri*, and this one, an atheistic Jewish lawyer, ended up as a student in Farel House (the name of the study section of *L'Abri*) for six months. A common factor in every case, however, for those of us who comprise the Workers of *L'Abri*, is this: we believe that God brings the people in answer to prayer. As definite, believing prayer is made that God will bring the people of His choice to us, and keep all others away, we believe that this prayer has been, and is being, answered.

What are they doing there?

If they are guests they are simply listening to some of the lectures or discussions on tapes with earphones or in groups, or they are having personal conversations with some of the workers, or they are taking part in asking questions as they sit around the fireplace on a Saturday evening, or around meal tables three times a day, in family settings. If they have come to be Farel House students, they pursue their course (set individually for each one by Dr. Schaeffer), listening to lectures, discussions, sermons and Bible studies for four hours each morning, each one with earphones and an individual tape-recorder. There are two "live lectures" a week and seminar periods, as well as Sunday services, high tea and Bible study on Sunday evenings. There are occasional musical evenings, with wonderful solos by the *L'Abri* worker who was formerly an opera singer, and others contributing their talents—violin, piano, organ, cello, and so forth.

The really basic thing they have in common in what they are doing is that each one has come with a *need*—a personal need, or a need to be prepared to help others in the midst of the chaos of the twentieth-century intellectual climate, and they are seeking answers at *L'Abri*. In addition to time spent in conversation, tape listening or lectures, half the day is spent entering into the practical work in a family setting.

How is all this financed?

The factual human answer is that gifts come in from many different places, and are placed in a general fund out of which rents, mortgage payments and electric bills are paid, and the housekeepers are given money for food. No one asks anybody to give money, however. No pleas are made to human beings or organisations, and no pledges are asked for. Guests and helpers at *L'Abri* do *not* pay anything, and all expenses for them are met out of the general fund. Farel House students pay $1.50 (about 13 shillings) a day for food, and $0.50 (or just over 4 shillings) a day for the repair of tape-recorders, heating and other expenses connected with Farel House. Workers get no salary, but give themselves to this work, receiving their basic needs. If there is enough money, a gift of about $30 (about £10) is received by each Worker each month. The budget is a "shoe string" one for all the people who come and go, who live at *L'Abri*, travel to teach classes and so on. Those of us who are Workers at *L'Abri* believe that this money comes in as an answer to specific prayer for the needs.

What is the stated purpose of L'Abri?

We have established our purpose as this: "To show forth by

demonstration, in our life and work, the existence of God."
We have in other words decided to live on the basis of prayer
in several realms, so that we might demonstrate to any who
care to look the existence of God. We have set forth to live by
prayer in these four specific realms:

1. We make our financial and material needs known to God
alone, in prayer, rather than sending out pleas for money.
We believe that He can put it into the minds of the people of
His choice the share they should have in the work.

2. We pray that God will bring the people of His choice to
us, and keep all others away. There are no advertising leaflets,
and this book is the first to be written about the work.

3. We pray that God will plan the work, and unfold His plan
to us (guide us, lead us) day by day, rather than planning
the future in some clever or efficient way in committee
meetings.

4. We pray that God will send the workers of His choice
to us, rather than pleading for workers in the usual channels.

In the eleven years now since *L'Abri* started, the work has
grown from one small family living in Chalet les Mélèzes,
praying and receiving people, to the complex of chalets, and
the chapel, described here. Also there is *L'Abri* work in Milan,
London, and Amsterdam, and there are representatives in
America. It must be emphasised, however, that just as there
have been no appeals for money, or advertising for workers,
guests or students, so there has been no intention to make a big
organisation of *L'Abri*. The number of those actually engaged
in the work (Members and Workers as they are called) is very
small indeed, and it is this group alone that makes up the
organisation of *L'Abri*.

Whether we be large or small, widely known or less widely
known, our prayer has been simply to fulfil God's purpose faith-
fully. In fact, the work and the teaching *have* become known
more widely, so that Dr. Schaeffer and others in the work are
now receiving many more requests than can possibly be accepted from theological seminaries, university groups, schools and
colleges, churches, and non-Christian groups all over the world.
The interest and eagerness with which people from the most

16

diverse strata of thought and backgrounds are either coming to *L'Abri*, or inviting the Schaeffers to speak, is remarkable.

The story which follows is one in which the author has attempted to show the reality of the fact that God exists, and that He is the One who has, time after time, answered prayer in the midst of well-nigh impossible circumstances to bring about something out of nothing.

Temple Protestant, Champéry

CHAPTER ONE

It couldn't happen in Switzerland

IT WAS Valentine's Day 1955 and Susan and Debby had decorated a box with red hearts and lace and had filled it with hand-painted cards with original rhymes to be read aloud at the appropriate moment. Many were the muffled giggles coming from their corner of the dining-room as ideas were being exchanged and plans for games were being invented. Smells of baking chocolate cake drifted out from the kitchen where two heart-shaped layers were rising in the oven of the newly installed American electric stove, and where the ingredients were being assembled for a pink peppermint icing. It seemed like a perfect moment for a celebration. Little Franky was falling less now, as he learned to cope with his partially paralysed leg (left that way from the polio attack which hit him five months before, the last night we were on the boat in the midst of travel back to Switzerland from America)... and Susan was up again after her first attack of rheumatic fever.

The house itself seemed to need a celebration to give it proper recognition for its having just emerged from a cocoon of drabness into a transformed "night moth" of beauty ... for we had just completed painting the kitchen, installing electrical equipment, scraping old cracked plaster from one corner of the dining-room so that the original stone could be enjoyed, and remaking saggy, raggy furniture into "almost new" with fabrics picked the year before at an interior decorator's in the States.

Yes, Chalet Bijou at last looked almost as it had been visualised in vivid imaginations for years—"once we get it fixed up". There was nothing left to do to it but to put cherry red linoleum on the splintery hall floors . . . and that had already been measured, ordered, and was going to be laid any day now!

Another cause for a happy family celebration was the fact that we felt the need of a bit of relaxation after the most recent ordeal. Only a few weeks before this, avalanches had come tearing down the mountainside right at our chalet . . . missing it only by a few *feet*.

Let me describe the avalanches. We had had wonderful days of "good snow" and that gorgeous mid-winter Alpine sunshine that makes ski-ing in Switzerland something very special. "Fran",[1] Priscilla and Debby had skied whenever they could fit it in . . . in between tears, dinners and evenings during which we all concentrated on cooking, serving, keeping Franky quiet in the background, or talking to people. Conversations were important to us, because people usually came to visit us with serious questions to ask: people at hotels for ski-ing, who had attended our Sunday chapel service, or students who had been at Chalet Bijou for evenings when they had been with their boarding schools in Champéry . . . and now had come back for the holidays with friends. It was the season when the phone rang often, and teatime ran into dinner time, and dinner time blended into an evening of conversation with refreshments served.

As I was saying, we had the kind of weather hotels hope for in ski resorts. Caroline, an English girl who had come to study the Bible with us for a couple of weeks, was leaving on a Wednesday, and I remember that that Monday she stayed up at Planachaux ski-ing all afternoon, coming home with sunburned nose, tanned cheeks and a ravenous appetite, for supper. Tuesday we were all glad she had taken her ski trip on Monday, for we awakened to the noise of rain drumming on the roof. It was a good day for staying indoors and finishing up all the questions she had hoped to ask before leaving. Wednesday, when we found it was still raining, we decided her

---

[1] Francis Schaeffer—my husband.

bag should be taken to the station in the afternoon, because simply walking there without bags would be a "feat" in itself in the dark. Both Fran and I went up with her to the train that night, slipping and sliding over the fields, which were now lakes of water on top of ice.

"I'll never be able to thank you people enough for all these weeks have meant to me. It has been the most important time of my life," said Caroline formally, in between pants as she struggled to get up a hill on the slippery wet ice. The rain had drenched us all by now, and yet the water streaming down from Caroline's hair and dripping off her chin, plus the puffing and panting as we struggled to make headway uphill, did *not* detract from the solemnity of the occasion. With the suitcase and bulging rucksack hurriedly pushed up beside her, and skis balanced on her shoulders, she waved good-bye, and assured us she was going to send friends along to Bijou . . . friends who needed to know "truth". We slid our way back, each thinking our own thoughts about the future, wondering how our work and lives would develop.

Early the next morning we awakened to the sounds of muffled talking coming from outside, excited voices coming from Priscilla's room, the steady roar of the torrent coming down the stream bed beside the chalet, and rain on the roof. What could be going on? I slipped out of bed and into Priscilla's room to find her and Susan both peering intently out of the window. . . .

"Look, Mommy, the torrent is *full* because of all the rain and melting snow . . . and lots of logs have backed up against our bridge and the whole thing has overflowed. Look out here, it looks like a lake . . . they've been here ever so long digging ditches to carry the water away from the house, and taking the bridge apart and fishing logs and stones out of the stream. Why doesn't Daddy go out and work too?"

"Daddy" didn't know this was going on, as nothing had awakened us on that side of the house, but soon he had stuck on some old clothes and was out in the pouring rain with a shovel and rake. Susan looked like Eliza crossing the ice as she picked her way through the water with a tray full of cups of hot coffee from time to time throughout the morning, serving Rachel, Hermann and Robert (the Swiss peasant brothers and sister who owned our chalet) as well as her daddy and a man from across the fields as they worked to try to direct the water back into the regular stream bed. At noon Fran came in to eat, change soaked clothes, and then to leave for the village. . . .

"They need help up in the village as several of the other torrents are in danger of jumping their beds . . . and new torrents are coming down where no stream has ever been before."

Bridges were all down, and only one plank was laid across each place where crossing was necessary. Clusters of men stood at each place where a torrent crossed the village street . . . each with a shovel keeping the stones and mud cleared away so that the water would *keep* going down. At suppertime Fran came home to change clothing, eat, and then to go back for the "night shift".

That night avalanches began to make their way down the mountainside with frightening rushes. We could hear the roar at our chalet. As mud, stones, branches and trees swept everything along with them, suddenly the stability of man-made houses—the permanent appearance of the old village—seemed as nothing more than a child's building of blocks. Sudden destruction seemed very possible with the shifting, unpredictable earth . . . and we realised in a very vivid way that only an all-powerful God could be depended upon to take care of "all our needs".

The new day was Friday, and the rain had been coming without a stop since Monday. In the afternoon Fran and I walked up to the village to see how things were going. Two chalets had been hit and the foundations were sticking out crookedly beyond the house. One barn had collapsed entirely, just after the sheep and horses had been removed. The street was full of mud and stones—six feet deep in some places. All the stores had a pitifully small protection of sandbags and planks across the windows and a small bulldozer was removing deep mud from in front of one store. We went up as far as the Marclays' house (our first landlord and his wife, still our good friends) crossing two torrents that had never been there before, and inspected the avalanche that had just missed our church. As we came across the fields toward Chalet Bijou we saw Madame Fleischmann in front of us . . . a village man helping her to carry her belongings. Madame Fleischmann is a lovely German lady who lived in a tiny two-room chalet perched on a steep slope. She had been ordered to evacuate because of two dangerously near torrents tearing down past her "doll's-house" home. She had her feather bed, a suitcase of important papers, a suitcase of valuables and a bag full of food so that she could continue her special diet! She sank down gratefully to rest in the room where she was installed and sighed, "No avalanche could ever reach us here . . . there is so much field between you and the mountains."

I patted her on the shoulder, and went down to prepare supper, since meals had to continue, as did Franky's daily treatment for polio.

Supper over, Madame Fleischmann went off to bed where she felt safe enough to sleep, "so far removed from danger". Fran went back to the village to continue shovelling, and Helen and Priscilla decided to take flashlights and cross the fields to satisfy their curiosity as to what was going on. (Helen was my Swiss *sage-femme* when Franky was born, and had come back for a visit.) Enormous searchlights had been set up on the village tennis courts by soldiers sent by the State to help in the emergency so the whole mountainside was lit up in an attempt to see any beginning of a new avalanche so that people might flee in time. Men were stationed at various places higher up the mountain and as they signalled with flashlights it was hard not just to stay by a window to watch the drama, fascinating in spite of its terrifying qualities. We were doing just this— Susan, Debby and I—when we saw the bobbing flashlights announcing Helen and Priscilla's return across the fields. Suddenly as they were nearing the chalet, a great roaring *shout* went up from the darkness of the fields and road above the circle of their small lights, "ATTENTION . . . ATTENTION . . . C'EST ICI . . . C'EST ICI!"

The girls stopped in their tracks, turned to see what it

might be—and then they broke into a wild run for the chalet screaming, "*C'est ici*—it's coming HERE—it's coming HERE!"

Electric lights had been strung from our house to a tree by the torrent to facilitate work in case the torrent flooded again, and in this light I could see an oozing, writhing mass of mud slithering toward us, as wide as the whole field, and in the mud there seemed to be a host of little streams. By the time I had run downstairs and outside, Robert had arrived looking like a wild man. Fear seemed to have frozen his tongue and he just grunted when I spoke to him. The only thing I could think of doing was to drag planks from the former bridge and try to protect the chalet's foundations with them. We *had* no sandbags.

Priscilla was tugging away at planks, too, and we tried to make a barricade which would turn the mass of mud in another direction. However, many of our boards just went floating merrily away like leaves thrown on a stream. Rachel and Hermann appeared on the scene with shovels and more planks, and Fran suddenly came into sight, having jumped and waded across a torrent in spite of the protests of the men, endangering himself . . . because this was a *real* avalanche and enormous stones (the size of a dining-room table) were coming down right where he crossed over.

Helen was telephoning the village for more help . . . and then she called *Ecole Biblique* in Geneva to ask for special prayer. Susan and Debby had been told to take some of the things from the first floor (files, books, etc.) upstairs, and I came in to find Susan dashing upstairs with my best tea set, removing it from a top shelf to "save it". Many weird things were being dragged off upstairs by this army of two! Now the boards had given out, so someone went up into the attic and began passing our packing case wood down—and poor Madame Fleischmann was up once more acting as part of a chain to pass the wood downstairs.

What a night it was! Barricades were made and no water came into the house, though muddy boots brought enough of the mud in to cover the floors. We discovered later that the avalanche had started to come down in the torrent bed, then it had jumped the torrent far up above, spreading out over the fields and coming towards our house. However, a few hundred feet above us, the central force of water and the enormous rocks and stones crossed the torrent to the opposite side, and came straight down the path on the *other* side of our bridge. The field over there was full of enormous stones, and the water had cut a deep gully where our path had been—but our chalet was spared. We had deep mud and smaller stones all around us, but nothing big enough to break the foundations. Our feverish attempts to "protect" the place made about as much sense as Debby and Susan's ineffectual "saving" of the family possessions.

The days that followed were one jumble of muddy floors, soaked clothing, meals served in between coffee being handed out to the outdoor workers, dark settling down too soon every day . . . making a nightmare out of the always-present dangers. Searchlights scanning the mountainside all night, men flashing lights (which Susan was constantly interpreting as a signal that new avalanches were coming!) as they patrolled the heights above, the noise of the roaring torrents, the never-ending rain and winds, the need to keep our torrent clear of stones and branches which might stop it up and cause another flood, and the straining of one's ears for the village church bell (which gave the announcement of further disasters)—all of this made it impossible to get any consecutive sleep. We kept dressed because it was prudent to do so in case of need for sudden evacuation. Fran and Priscilla spent one entire day clearing the torrent, and making a new barricade—and he took his shift on the village street, too. The danger lasted for over a week.

Immediately after that time the days became full again with our normal rush of writing, caring for the needs of those who came seeking help, and the day by day needs of the convalescents.

Now it was Valentine's Day—time for a family evening to mark the end of a disrupted period, and the beginning of a more normal one—and we were all looking forward to it with a sigh of relief.

Suddenly the phone rang. "The village gendarme would

like Daddy to come up right away. He has something that would 'interest him' concerning our *permis de séjour*."

"Come along with me, Priscilla, I may need you for translation."

So off went Fran and Priscilla while the rest of us went on with what we were doing—more or less, that is, as there was a feeling of apprehension because we had returned from America the first week in September, and the permits should have been given us *long* ago.

We saw them coming back through the fields. Fresh snow had turned the torn up fields into strange lumpy affairs with rocks still showing through at spots, with branches and broken trees strewn like matchsticks, spoiling the usual perfection of the view. Regret over the spoiled view was soon to be a minor thought pushed out of the mind. A cold air blew in as they opened the kitchen door and stamped their feet on the cement floor.

"Mother, Mother, you can't imagine what has happened."
"Here, Edith, read these . . ."

I took the two sheets of paper, printed forms, filled in with typed bits, reading the orange one first, which was marked "Sion".

"Monsieur and Madame Schaeffer, Priscilla, Susan and Deborah must leave Champéry, and the Canton of Valais by midnight the night of March 31" . . .

"Why, that's six weeks from now? Six weeks? We have to *leave*!"

I read on, finding the reason given as this: "having had a religious influence in the village of Champéry". The children were exclaiming now with excited voices.

"Shhhh . . . let me read the other one" (the white one).

"Monsieur and Madame Schaeffer, Priscilla, Susan and Deborah must leave all of Switzerland by midnight the night of March 31, not to return for the space of two years."

And the same reason was given on this paper from Berne: "having had a religious influence in the village of Champéry".

"But it isn't possible," we exclaimed in dismay.

"It *couldn't* happen in Switzerland."

CHAPTER TWO

A New Beginning

IT WAS in September 1948 that we had first arrived as a
family in Switzerland. I remember my feeling as we stepped
out of the taxi at La Rosiaz, and lined up on the side-
walk—three little girls dressed alike in plaid gingham dresses
and navy blue coats, Fran and myself, waiting for the luggage
to be unloaded.

"Oh, the *air*," I thought, "the clean, clean air . . . why it's
as if the windows had suddenly been washed, and you'd forgotten how dirty they were. I didn't realise there could be *this*
much difference in air."

It was tremendous to breathe, the sun felt different coming
through it . . . and what a clarity it gave to the view!

"*Bonjour, Madame; bonjour, Monsieur; bonjour, mes enfants,
bonjour, bonjour.*"

Madame Turrian, who ran Pension Riant Mont, and her
two Swiss German girl helpers, picked up some of the luggage
and guided us up the steps which took us through an arch in
the retaining wall (which seemed designed to stop the garden
from falling into the street), up to the level of the house, then
on up winding stone stairs to the third floor.

"*Voilà.*"

And there we were. Our new home! Two small bedrooms,
each with a tiny iron-railed balcony; one with twin beds, an
"armoire" (movable wooden cupboard in which to hang

clothes), a cupboard with four shelves in it, a table and one chair, two bedside tables each with a drawer and a square space under that, and a washbasin with a mirror over it. No chest of drawers, no dressing-table, no space even to walk around, much less to put more furniture. The second one had a single bed, a day-bed, a wooden crib . . . all with the huge feather-bed puffs on them. The rest of the room was the same as the first one.

We looked at each other in dismay. Where would the contents of the suitcases fit in? Where could toys be put? What about projector, screen and a suitcase full of slides? Where would typewriters be put, and files, paper, carbon and all the office equipment? Where could school books, Sunday school materials and drawing things go? Where could children study and play?

We had not come as tourists. This was not a vacation, nor an educational "year abroad" . . . but Fran and I, Priscilla aged eleven, Susan, seven, and Debby, three, had left our thirteen-room home in St. Louis (which was the manse of the evangelical Presbyterian Church of which my husband had been the pastor) and had come to Europe because we felt God had guided us to do so. Fran had been a pastor for ten years, and the summer before had been asked to make a survey trip to study the condition of Protestant Christianity in Europe. He had visited thirteen countries in thirteen weeks, and had talked to leaders of evangelical Christianity in each of those countries. Among other results of that trip was our going through struggles of being "pulled in two directions", seeking God's guidance, and eventually coming to the conclusion that we were being led to walk away from our "secure" life—as well as home and possessions—and go to Europe.

It was right after the war, and Europe still bore its scars—war-damaged buildings, and people living under stringent conditions as far as home and food went. But that which had become a deep concern to us was not the result of physical bombs which had torn up and scattered orderly *matter* into rubble, but the philosophical and theological "bombs" which had torn up and scattered faith and orderly *thinking*. It was not only that theology and philosophy were denying the existence of a personal God such as the Bible sets forth as being really *there*—that has been loudly expressed for many years—but the alarming thing was the generation growing up to be taught that one might as well not even argue about what truth is, because "absolute truth" is non-existent . . . all things are "relative".

Religious freedom is important, but the word "Christianity" is frequently a clever mask used to cover up the age-old wrinkles of agnosticism. Just as Communism freely uses the word "democratic" as an adjective applying to its most *un*democratic teachings, so terminology in theological realms needs defining these days.

This is simply the germ of that which troubled us and gave us a "fire" within to do something about helping adults who might be confused in the midst of the clamour of voices in our day, and especially about children growing up with no freedom to choose . . . because they were not aware that any educated person could believe the Bible to be true, and had never heard the message of the Bible from a believing viewpoint.

The most precious thing a human being has to give is time. There is so very little of it, after all, in a life. Minutes in an hour, hours in a day, days in a week, weeks in a year, years in a life. It all goes so swiftly! And what has been done with it? A burning zeal to do something in the realm of art, of music, of other creative fields, of science, of medicine, of exploration, of just plain living—yet how much time is there to develop in one's chosen field and to accomplish anything that makes even a smudge of a difference? When one feels one has found something far more important than how to utilise a lifetime with some purpose, when one feels one has found an open door to eternity with endless time to spend and an unending purpose to spend it *for*, when one is certain one is in communication with the Person who makes all this possible, then the burning still is there . . . but it is in a desire to *share* this certainty.

"God's guidance." "God led us." What meaningless phrases these must be to anyone who thinks there is no God; or that if there is, He is not personal and so could not be contacted by any sort of real communication; and that if He could, He would surely not care about any such insignificant speck in the universe as one human being, and that human being's use of his hours, days and life; or if He spoke one could not understand Him anyway, as He is so absolutely different.

We used our challenged ingenuity to fit things into the two rooms, rather like pieces in a jigsaw puzzle. Boxes under the beds were wonderful storage places for whatever they needed to hide, depending on the time of day. When it was time for office hours out came the typewriter to be placed on the bedside table, out came the nail-keg leather-covered stool (which had travelled the ocean safely packed with an assortment of things). From under the washbasin out came boxes of paper, carbon, envelopes and letters to be answered. Later it all disappeared, and the room became a family sitting-room where books were being read out loud. True there was only one place to sit comfortably, and five of us were perched in various spots on the beds, but it was definitely home and not the office any longer. The same sort of thing took place in the children's room, with a wooden box under the washbasin doubling for a place for little Debby to stand on to brush her teeth, and a toy box—and many things under the beds in labelled boxes.

What the rooms lacked in space inside, was made up for by the view from the balcony. Every day there'd be a cry from someone, "Oh look—look—LOOK . . . before it's too late, the sun is perfect right *now*."

Sometimes it would be a sunset which had turned the clouds and lake into liquid gold, other times a dark red sun in a grey sky was leaving a dark red streak in the ripples of the lake. Once an umbrella of grey covered the whole lake and the French Alps on the other side . . . but allowed the sun to be mysteriously reflected in the lake below, with only a rim of apricot bordering the "umbrella". There were fabulous sunsets, as well as fabulous skies at night, filled with stars and rimmed with blue-white snow-covered mountain peaks. One step out on the balcony took one miles away! And always there were the glittering lights of Evian on the other side of the lake, which began to twinkle in a friendly way at dusk. These views were as comforting "warm packs" put on the gnawing pains of homesickness . . . homesickness not just for a place, but for all that "home" had been as a way of life.

Language was of course an immediate difficulty. None of us spoke French. The children were "dropped" into a small Swiss school where they trudged daily, with their French schoolbooks in bags on their backs. Priscilla was soon swamped with French . . . French verbs . . . grammar exercises . . . vocabulary, which she had to master before she could go into the other subjects—history, literature and so forth—with the children her own age. Susan at seven had just finished first grade in America and now simply started first grade in French where she learned to read (at first it was just pronouncing).

"Oh Mommy . . . I can't understand the children, and I can't understand the teacher, and *now* I can't even understand *myself*!"

Debby's problem was less acute as she only needed to learn the names of colours and shapes and so on in kindergarten. Our meals were also a problem. Susan hated the soups made with oatmeal, tapioca, or cream of wheat in them . . . and often sat stubbornly in front of an untouched bowl she had been told to eat, and which she later had to eat cold! There were other unfamiliar tastes . . . and because of our having just enough money to pay for our *pension* with nothing left over, we could not buy fruit and things to eat in between, so what was not found in the three meals a day, had to be done without. Each child had twenty centimes (about five American cents) a week for allowance, and they used to press their noses against the village stores throughout the week, choosing what they considered the best buy—always food.

Then there was the constant restriction of lively behaviour! The other occupants of the *pension* were all in their eighties or nineties, and jumping, laughing or quarrelling children were not long tolerated. Whenever any noise was being made, doors would open and a long hissing "Shhh" would echo in the halls. Three-year-old Debby, with her head of curls, domestic instincts, and love of being a part of things, fitted in beautifully with her old lady playmates, as they gave her bits of wool to knit, and let her sit in their circle. She also followed mama Turrian around the kitchen learning to cook, and, incidentally, learning French. Susan found her own original method of making some noise to satisfy her tomboy nature. We discovered after a couple of weeks of Susan's more satisfied expression of countenance that her oxfords were being parked by the front door each morning, as she donned a pair of wooden Dutch shoes (purchased as a souvenir in Holland), and clumped off to school.

"I can *jump* in them, and kick my heels, and make all kinds of noise in them," she said with glee, when we questioned her.

"And what do the other children think?"

"Oh, I don't know, and I don't care . . . they just follow me and yell things in French."

When the end of October came, Susan, sad about having no Hallowe'en, shut herself away from us all for a couple of hours very mysteriously. When we came up from dinner that night (the children had left the table early—with our permission!), we found all three with masks on of Susan's creation (Debby in her crib, as she had bronchitis). Our room was decorated and games had been crookedly made on the backs of old form letters (pin the nose on the pumpkin) with crayons. She had even gone into the nearby orchard and had picked up some hard little green apples which were floating in the washbasin "to bob for"!

We tried to make up to the children for the church life they were missing by having absolutely regular "services". On Sunday mornings we'd shove our two beds a foot or so towards the French doors leading to the balcony, fit in three straight chairs and the stool (so that we could just sit down with our knees against the beds) between the beds and the washbasin . . . and place a hymnbook on each chair. Fran would stand on the step leading to the balcony, and the four of us would sit in the row of chairs, with Bibles and hymnbooks, and a full length service complete with hymns, Scripture reading, and sermon took place. Sunday evenings we had a "young people's" service which the children took turns in leading. I taught a Sunday school for them with illustrations as carefully made as if for a class of thirty. And we took Saturday afternoon bicycle rides (for about two hours) and called it "Empire Builders'" meeting . . . similar to Girl Scouts!

That first winter an American divorcee and her two children came to our services, and later an Irishwoman among the ninety-year-old group came up each Sunday, and an English nursemaid working for a family in Lausanne came out on the tram. In spite of this effort to make things more normal, our own nagging, discouraging thoughts were voiced by Priscilla one day as she wailed, "What are you *doing* here . . . why did we *come*? At home Daddy was preaching to a church full of people, and Mommy you were taking care of a whole big house, and teaching classes, and making all kinds of things for children's Bible illustrations . . . and . . . and . . . here you're just typing letters . . . and Daddy had a secretary at home to type for him. What are we doing over *here*?"

Chalet des Frênes, Champéry

CHAPTER THREE

Champéry

WHAT WERE we doing? That winter in Lausanne was spent in making contacts by correspondence, making a small start in studying French, talking with some individuals and groups in Switzerland, and making two speaking trips to Holland. I had, only shortly before, started taking a correspondence course in shorthand and typing, so my first weeks as a secretary were ones of working very slowly and painstakingly, but gradually I picked up speed so that more was accomplished in less time.

We began a pattern of trips that year, which continued throughout the next five years. We would usually stay two nights in one town, speaking in the same church two nights in succession. Fran would give a talk on "The History of the Church" from the early Church, in the Book of Acts in the Bible, down to the present day, in an outline form, of course. He would show how simple the early Church worship was, and how Roman Catholicism arose at the time of Constantine, and then give a summary of the Reformation and its going back to the two "pillars", (1) a non-humanist authority, which the Bible gives—an authority outside of man's relativistic thinking; and (2) a non-humanist approach to the absolute Holy God, upon the basis of the *finished, absolute* work of Christ upon the cross in space, and time and history. Then he would show how German Higher Criticism came into the Protestant church about two hundred years ago, and would explain how this destroyed the faith of many theological leaders and pastors in the inerrancy of the Bible, setting forth also the teaching that Jesus was not virgin-born and so forth, and was only a great example. He would then go on and show how Barthianism—the more modern and more subtle deviation from the Bible—arose, and something of its basic division of truth, as it states that there can be something that is "spiritually true but historically false" at the same time. This lecture of his on "The History of the Church" gave a background upon which he could speak of the confusion of our present day, and the need for clear understanding and teaching on the part of those who really do believe there is an absolute to teach, and a certainty to share in unfolding the Bible as the Word of the Living God.

Our second evening would be spent first by Fran speaking of the fact that the *children* are the ones who really have no opportunity to decide for themselves what truth is because the majority of them are not reading, or being taught the Bible at all; certainly not having it presented by anyone who believes it to be true. The teaching that the Bible is myth, is just as dogmatic, after all, as the dogmatic teaching of it as history! And the dogmatism most children are exposed to is a negative dogmatism. We would suggest how any women who were serious about this might teach the children of the neighbourhood in which they lived. I then gave a sample class—singing illustrated songs, telling a Bible story illustrated with pictures placed on a flannelboard, and giving object lessons to illustrate central teachings.

As the months went on Fran and I began to write lessons for the classes which were commencing, and eventually the lessons were translated and used in thirteen languages—having been translated and mimeographed by groups or individuals within the various countries.

This was one portion of our work, and it began during the year in Lausanne—though at times we felt the discouragement ourselves which Priscilla had put into words. As summer drew near, our French teacher urged us to go to the mountains. "All

Swiss do. It is important for the children's health to have a change in altitude," she said.

I took a trip to the village she suggested, Champéry, and visited one or two chalets which were for rent, selecting a lovely one full of balconies and geranium window-boxes, right next door to the Marclays, who owned it. The chalets were perched side by side on a steep slope, looking as if they should have giant ski sticks to hold on to, to prevent their sliding down! A small path went by our back door, and wound on up the mountain behind us. The rent, plus food costs, would amount to about the same as we paid at the *pension*, so I signed a contract.

You can imagine the children's delight at being in a whole house, "with Mommy in the kitchen," Susan squealed, in anticipation of tasting her favourite cooking once more. Now we had quite a different view, as Champéry is in a high bowl, 3,200 feet high, but with mountains of 6,000 to 10,400 feet towering above it on three sides, and a sharp drop to a river racing over rocks following the valley down on the open side. We looked out of windows now to see the mountains directly across from us, looking at waterfalls and cliffs rather than peaks or sky. It was necessary to go out to the balcony to see the sky and it seemed more like a ceiling stretched across from peak to peak, than the wide familiar sky in other surroundings. Now cooking, housekeeping and marketing were added to the secretarial work and care of the children.

Almost immediately visitors began to arrive for afternoon tea, and conversations. The first were some English schoolgirls Priscilla had met at the swimming pool, and invited for an afternoon. A teacher came with them. I used the opportunity to show them our "children's materials"—not that I expected them to use them, but because I wanted to say something to them without preaching. They were intensely interested, and later came back bringing more girls. This sort of thing continued throughout the summer. Fran made one trip to Holland alone. I spent one day answering a call for us to speak to a campful of young people in another part of Switzerland. Then Fran was called to London. And so the summer passed, and it came time to go back to Lausanne again.

Just before our return something happened which was a thread which would appear several times in the weaving of our lives in the next years. That "something" was a person by the name of Baroness von Dumreicher, who was staying with some young people in Chalet Bijou. A German baroness, she had spent forty years of her life in Egypt, and, as she said, they were years spent in light social pleasures. Many tragic things happened to different members of her family, and last of all her husband was killed, and she lost all her earthly possessions. She was living in Switzerland on money given her by a nephew, but it made her feel like a pauper. Troubled in her thoughts about the present and the future, she had heard of us, and asked us to visit her. Her first and most important desire was to know whether there was any way she could be assured that her sins would be forgiven. That there was an existing God, she had no doubt, but she feared death, and looked back on an empty life, filled with what she honestly felt was sin—and knew there was not much "time left to make up for it". With her earphone held out eagerly to catch every word she came step by step into that happy assurance which the Bible gives to believers, and which is not based on works which men must have *time* to do, but upon something that has been done for them by the Son of God. It is really an exciting thing to have a message like this for the world. If "eternal life" depended on what a person had time left to do, or strength to do, or will-power to do, or emotions to feel, or talent to accomplish, or brilliance to understand, or money to pay for, or family line or merit, how sad a thing it would be to say to such an eager searching question: "Sorry, but this is not for you."

As it was, the baroness became a Christian, and was as excited as a child finding hidden treasure.

"Why," said one of the young people to us, at the fruit store the next day, "she was so *changed*, and as happy as a child, and so pleased that it all happened on her birthday."

We began to see the return of the goats, sheep and cows from the higher mountain pastures, and chalets changed hands from summer visitors to village people who had spent the summer on the high alps. The fields nearby became filled with a symphony of bells of all sizes from the tiny ones on the sheep to the largest ones of the cows, all ringing with different tones. The children thrilled at the "Switzerland of Heidi", and begged to live permanently in the village. . . .

"Why do we have to go back?"

We realised that there was no real reason, except one of convenience for travel, the name of a larger town as an address, and the release for me from housework to be secretary. However, some inquiries gave us the information that chalets are rented by the year at a much cheaper price than for the season, and by doing a bit of arithmetic I discovered that with the cheaper chalet rent, we could afford some household help . . . and then perhaps it could be done!

Madame Marclay regretted that her chalet was already rented for the winter, so if anything were to be found, it would have to be within a few days, as almost everything had already been taken for the winter ski season. We prayed, "Dear Heavenly Father, if it be Thy will for us to live in this village, please show us a suitable chalet this week, and a school for the children."

We found the school the next day. Home Eden, a *pension* for children who needed mountain air for some reason, had about twelve children living there. The two Swiss ladies who ran it seemed not only capable, but real characters.

"Why, Mother," said Susan excitedly after her first days there, "it's like a story book! The teacher irons, mends the children's clothing, and does embroidery while she drills them in arithmetic . . . and she's a good teacher too."

This *pension* made an exception to their rule that they only took boarders, and let Susan and Debby come as day pupils, since we were going to be leaving them whenever we went on speaking trips to other countries. For Priscilla, who needed a more advanced education, we found a boys' boarding school which took day pupils, and, making an exception, took her as the only girl! She stayed at Home Eden with the younger ones during our trips.

A chalet, however, did *not* turn up until the very last day . . . when we had almost given up. We met the sister of our French teacher on the village street. She stopped us and said, "I hear you want to rent a chalet. Well, I take care of one for an English family, and it is such a headache to clean it and prepare it for short times, such as summer, and then the winter ski season, that I would be glad to rent it for a whole year. You may have it for just the price of the two seasons, as it will be saving me work."

We went to see Chalet des Frênes and marvelled at what had been given to us—for it seemed to us a gift in answer to that prayer. It was a beautiful English country house, built in the style of a chalet, with central heating, gorgeous beamed living-room with a huge fireplace and built-in seats on two sides of it. It had a splendid garden, and even a summer house which the children claimed as their playhouse. Each of us could have our own rooms, and there was a room for an office and guest rooms besides. It was completely furnished even with sheets, silver, and cooking utensils. We took it, and had a time of thanksgiving!

We had promised Madame Turrian we would come back, and we kept our promise, telling her that we would not leave until the end of October, and that we would pray that her rooms would be rented by then. Susan went scouting for applicants. She stopped likely looking older ladies on the street and said, "It's a *very* good *pension* with *wonderful* soup, for ladies like you." (Her previous loud complaints and stubbornness over the soup had always brought forth exclamations from the ladies as to how good the soup was!)

Madame Turrian did have the rooms rented before we left, and on 2nd November 1949 we moved to Champéry, bag and baggage, trunks and crates. Such an excitement as there was over unpacking things that had been stored for two years—especially the books. Loud whoops met the unearthing of each familiar book, with shouts of: "Oh, I *love* that book . . . here let me read it to you."

We were soon settled in, with our new schedule suited to life in a home rather than a boarding house . . . but not anticipating any change in our basic work. We had speaking trips already planned, and the first one was within a few days, to

Paris; others later on took us to the four Scandinavian countries, and eventually we went as far south as Spain and Portugal. In each of the countries children's classes were started, and an individual, or a group, took charge of translating lessons.

We were preparing the living-room for our family Christmas, expecting to have it two days early, because of guests coming for a two-week stay on Christmas Eve, and in the midst of our tying ornaments on the dark, fragrant branches of a freshly-cut tree brought from the forests above, the doorbell rang. A dark-haired, French-speaking young pastor was ushered in. I stayed out of sight of the visitor, since I had to care for cookies that were baking, prepare supper, and run to the village for more groceries.

It wasn't long, however, before an excited Susan swished into the kitchen to report the visitor's errand, and then swished out again. It seemed he had come to visit the few Protestants in town. While visiting, he met a director of a girls' school, there for the holiday season, who asked if there would be a Christmas service in English for Protestants. The pastor could not speak English, and there was not a Protestant service of any kind at that time in this Roman Catholic village in a Roman Catholic *canton*. (There are twenty-two *cantons*, some of which are Roman Catholic, and the others Protestant.)

Someone present during his meeting with the school director told him that there was an American Protestant pastor living in Chalet des Frênes.

But if we were to have services, where could they be held? It seems an Englishwoman who always spent her vacations in Champéry, had built a chapel, back in 1912, a lovely stone building, with gothic ceiling in dark wood, and cream coloured walls. It had green and brown scripture texts on the walls at that time, in French. Apparently she was a person who believed the Bible and felt this would be something she could do for this place she loved. She had died sometime before, and had left the building in the hands of a committee in another part of Switzerland. The chapel stood empty most of the time. It would be available for a Christmas service, if someone would provide wood for a fire! The village hairdresser's wife was discovered to be a Protestant, and one who could play the little pump organ, so all plans were settled.

Debby stood on her head on the couch and sang happily . . . "Daddy is going to preach in a really, truly church with lots of people there. I can't 'member a really, truly church with Daddy preaching."

I don't know who was the happiest member of the family! Fran himself went off to study the notes of the sermon he had thought he was preaching for our little family service, and I felt as if I were floating down to the store a few minutes later.

To understand our joy in this, you have to understand that we *believe* that the message of the Bible, so wrapped up in the Christmas message, is really true and a matter of "life and death" importance.

It was icy cold as we hurried down the street on Christmas Sunday, though there was no snow. The sun was gilding the snow above us as it hit the peaks of the Dents du Midi before pushing above the mountains far enough to bathe the village in its warmth for a few short hours.

Debby stamped her feet to warm up her toes, in between little skipping steps. "Who will come to the church to hear Daddy preach?" she asked.

I couldn't help an expectant shiver as I wondered whether *anyone* would come. A moment's glance as we entered the cold building (a small wood stove belching forth little puffs of smoke was the only sign of heat) gave us our answer. Filling whole pews were methodical rows of schoolchildren! There was one group of identically dressed girls, prim in navy blue, from a London school, there for two weeks of ski-ing; another of kilt-clad Scottish boys; and other groups hemmed in by teachers, obviously on vacation trips from England. There were also some from Swiss schools, and individuals from hotels. Altogether, there must have been about a hundred and fifty people. A silent prayer went up that we might have opportunity to talk to some of these people personally, rather than just having them drift out and away, without our knowing whether they had particular problems.

After the service was over, Susan bounded out happily to

where I was standing, and whispered loudly to me, "There's a man and lady talking to Daddy about could we have another service next week."

Face beaming, Susan bounded in again, not wanting to miss anything. Permission had to be sought from the committee, and rather than giving permission for "one more service" they replied that they would be glad to have us use the church for anything we would like to use it for, "as long as you live in Champéry".

Regular Sunday morning services were added to our schedule, and I had the fun of sketching, and printing by hand, twenty-two posters to put in the various hotels and *pensions*, announcing a church service in English, at the "Temple Protestant" near the railroad station. The hotel-keepers were pleased to have one more "provision" for the tourists, especially at no cost to the village! We were thanked by the *pensions* too, where school groups would be staying, and we were told of various ones coming for winter sports. When we spoke to a Christian businessman in Lausanne about the commencement of these regular services he was amazed. "And I thought you'd be burying yourselves in Champéry . . . and now this! It really is a remarkable opportunity."

We soon discovered that among the English-speaking people at the services were girls who came regularly week by week, and who said they were in a Finishing School which had rented a hotel, and would be staying in Champéry until March. Most Swiss schools which have an international group of young people in them—and all the "Finishing School" type of schools—go to a ski resort and rent a large chalet or hotel for the winter season. The whole staff goes along, and school lessons are done in the morning, while ski lessons are given on the sunny slopes in the afternoon (or vice versa!).

An invitation was given to some of the girls as they stood talking at the back of the church to "come to our chalet this Thursday night for an informal evening of conversation and tea. Bring any questions you might have concerning religion, or the Bible, or just anything that troubles you."

They accepted enthusiastically, but later in the week we

were disappointed by a call from the Director, Monsieur F., who said rather coolly that the girls had come for the purpose of ski-ing and studying . . . that's *all* . . . and could not come. This seemed final.

That same week we had a splendid talk with the doctor from Monthey who came to visit Susan, who had complained of an ache in her knee. He evidently liked us as much as we liked him, because we found later that he had talked enthusiastically about us to the Director of the girls' school—Monsieur F. We soon received an invitation to have dinner at the school (Fran and I), and to show coloured slides of European countries to the girls. That evening Monsieur F. was delighted with the slides, and kept saying, "The girls ought to see more of these . . ." To which we replied that we'd be glad to have them come to the chalet any time! The result was that a *general* invitation was given, and rather than the half dozen who would have come from the first invitation, thirty-two turned up! There were Zoroasterists from India, Buddhists from Siam, and girls of various backgrounds of religious or anti-religious views from England, Canada, Argentina, Haiti, Denmark, Scotland, America and Czechoslovakia. We had a most stimulating evening, which started with slides being shown, tea and cakes served, and ended with more serious questions.

That was the first of many such nights—the only changes being that we soon dropped the custom of starting with slides, because everyone wanted more time for questions.

One morning the six o'clock darkness found us making our way to the station for the 6.17 train to Lausanne, which (with changes at Aigle) would get us there by 9 a.m. We were lugging a crate back, to get the refund on it, and Fran and Debby had decided to ride astride the crate fixed on top of a suitcase, on a "luge" (or sled). I was coming along more demurely at a dog trot, to save snagging my nylon stockings! Debby was going to visit her elderly playmates, and we were going to do "101 things", including a visit to dear old Baroness von Dumreicher.

"Where haff you bean?" she asked reproachfully. "I haff so

moch to talk to you about. Come sit here." She held her "teapot" to her ear and settled down into her big chair with a shawl drawn around her shoulders. (Her "teapot", by the way, was what she called her ear trumpet, because a waiter once took it away and placed it among the teapots!) We had dinner with her, and she told us of all her many troubles.

Then, "But I must tell you about the dear boy who has been so kind to me . . ." and the next few hours of conversation were interspersed with descriptions of Christian D., a great tall Norwegian medical student who had been coming to help to cheer her up.

"He lives in a little room, cooks his own food, mends his own socks, washes and irons for himself, and helps his land-lady in part payment for his room. He comes when I'm sick and fixes my pillows for me, and fixes me a cup of tea. He talks very slowly, and never unless he really has something to say. Ha! Are you becoming interested in him?"

We were. Fran asked if he would enjoy a weekend with us in the mountains.

"Ach, that would do him moch good. But how moch would it cost?"

Fran answered by handing her the money for the car fare and saying, "Tell him it is in part payment for all the Nor-wegians did for me when I was sick in Oslo . . . and ask him to come to us for the weekend."

I wish I could describe that whole weekend in detail to you. Champéry was decorated with flags for a sports fête, and fresh snow added to the festive air as well as to the beauty. The children ran to meet Christian on the road from the station, and brought him to the kitchen door in their haste to get him into the house. Six foot six, Norwegian blue eyes, and a thatch of light hair had made him easy to recognise.

"Oh, it's just like home, you don't know," he said, and he proceeded to fit in as if it were!

He did everything from shovelling a walk to the street in the deepening snow, to washing dishes, and telling Norwegian fairy tales to the fascinated children around the fireplace, and taking the girls for a thrilling sled ride, the Norwegian way.

Priscilla described it as they came in with glowing cheeks and sparkling eyes: "We went way up the back road at least two miles, and he cut a long pole about twelve feet long, from a tree. He said to hold our feet up, and he did too (Swiss sleds are steered by putting one's heel down), and we just flew and flew . . . and he held the stick behind the sled, like a rudder on a boat, and steered with it. Wheee . . . I've never had a ride like that!"

Sunday we had the regular church service, and Christian came along. Then Sunday night he stood at the door, and took coats as the schoolgirls filed in, chattering and snowy, and it wasn't long before he discovered a Norwegian among them, and their chatter turned into Norwegian! The questions interested Christian, and after the girls left he asked a few more himself.

And so the first winter at Champéry began. We put off our Scandinavian trip until mid-March so that we could continue our times with the girls. Just before we left for Scandinavia, a wonderful thing happened—wonderful, that is to anyone who believes that Christianity *is* true—Christian, who had been an agnostic, became a Christian!

As we look back on it now, we had a "preview" in those first two months, of what was coming years later, but we had no idea of that. We only knew that our prayer for guidance had been answered, and that our coming to Champéry had far more purpose than just satisfying the children's longing for a home, and for a home in the charming "tucked in the mountains" village which Champéry is. We knew God had brought us there.

CHAPTER FOUR

Chalet Bijou

As WE prepared for our first long trip away from the children there were many tearing emotions at leaving them. I was thankful for their understanding of the purpose of our trips, and the feeling they had of sharing our sense of the importance of what we felt God had given us to do. That sharing showed up in their excitement over the news that Christian had become a Christian. They did not say, "but he was the nicest person we ever knew, so he must have been a Christian" . . . because they seemed really to understand that just being "nice" or having a charming personality or a sensitive, kind nature, is *not* the Bible's criterion of judgement of a man: it is whether he believes what God *says*. They also shared our happiness in the apparent results of the evening discussion groups with the girls, and were particularly pleased that blonde, tiny, Analie from Argentina had also come to believe.

When the "puffy lady" and "the teacher" (Susan's names for them) came from Home Eden to call on us, I showed them the Sunday school materials we were going to give Priscilla to teach her younger sisters during our absence.

"Could she have permission to have a class with her sisters on Sunday afternoon?" I asked.

"Oh, of course. In fact, the children at the pension are so eager to have Priscilla come back and tell them more stories, that I think it would be good if she would have *all* of them in a class." So Priscilla's training as a teacher commenced!

As the day of our leaving approached, I felt I just couldn't leave the children for seven weeks! But an idea came that helped *me* to walk away a bit more easily, and I hoped would bridge the first emptiness between the time they awakened to find us gone, and the time when someone would be coming to take them and their suitcases to the school. My last moment bright idea was placed at the foot of their beds, at the "wee hour" that found the packing finished! In the morning each one wakened to find gaily wrapped presents, which they ran to open together . . . so as we were on our way down the mountainside, they were having a kind of "second Christmas" before they dressed to go off to Home Eden for two months.

That trip, and the subsequent ones during the next years, would make a book in themselves, but they are not what I want to tell you in this story. Let me just say that the longer ones were timed so that we could be in Champéry when the winter and summer seasons brought people who were interested in church services. We were thrilled with the results. Children's classes called "Children for Christ" began in many places, and we were busy sending rolls of pictures to illustrate lessons we were writing (twenty-eight of them on the Book of Luke, for instance), and answering letters as they started to come in to us from the countries where we had been. The children shared a trip with us to Holland, and became the sample class as they sang the songs to illustrate a children's class; and Debby went with us on a trip visiting *Action Biblique* groups all over Switzerland (a fine Christian work centred in Geneva, with a Bible School there), where she enjoyed playing with toys brought out for her from attics and trunks at each home where we stayed, and helped us by singing children's songs at the meetings. The whole family went to Munich the next summer, to hold a two-week Bible School for children of American Army dependants.

It was during the Christmas season of 1950–1 that Susan came to me one day and said, "Mommy . . . you're going all over Europe to start children's Bible classes because it is so important for them to hear what the Bible says . . . and you— don't even have a class in your home."

She stood in front of me with her arms behind her back and pursed her lips dramatically, waiting for my answer.

"Well, Susan, we only came to Switzerland, and to this village, to live, not as missionaries to the country in that way."

"But the people you tell to have classes just have them in their homes wherever *they* live. What's the matter, are you *afraid*? You tell the Finnish people not to be afraid of the Russians, because God will take care of them . . . are *you* afraid?" She wasn't being saucy, just very much in earnest.

I took a deep breath and said, "Well Susan, I don't speak French well enough to teach a class."

Whereupon she quickly answered "Priscilla does . . . she could teach it, and you could help her ahead of time with the lesson."

It didn't seem right to give any more excuses when she went on with, "The children here *need* to know that their sins *can* be forgiven, and that Jesus really took all their punishment, and they don't *have* to be afraid of purgatory."

"All right, Susan, if Priscilla will teach, and if you will invite the children, and if the parents will let them come . . . you may have a class."

The Christmas class, with the Christmas story told by Priscilla in front of Chalet des Frênes' fireplace, and a treat of hot chocolate and cookies, with six children Susan had invited, was the children's first class, in their own first independent attempt to spread the truth to others! It became a regular weekly occurrence, and it grew steadily. Children came from children's *pensions*, as well as village homes, and eventually there were as many as twenty-five from the village school, as well as others. Priscilla did a good job of holding their attention with her natural story-telling talent, and of leading them in songs and drilling them in memorising verses. Each one took away a Bible verse printed by hand on some little "shape" or illustration of the day's story, cut out of coloured art paper, and these appeared on the walls of village homes, and even in the village school.

Debby had had her fifth birthday. During the day I found her standing on a chair intently examining her face in a mirror. "There isn't any difference," she said shaking her head. "There just isn't *any* difference than when I was *four*!"

Susan had had her ninth birthday exuberantly exclaiming all day, and for many days thereafter, "Oh I'm so *glad* I'm nine. I've been waiting all my life to be *nine*. You aren't little any more when you're nine."

And Priscilla had entered into the magic circle of the teenagers as she had her thirteenth birthday—with one big regret: "Oh, Mother, I wish I had *girls* to go to school with. I've always wanted to be a teenager, but I want a girl to *share* it with . . . my own age."

Her wish came true in a most amazing way. But it was more than a wish, because we had very definitely prayed, asking God to give us a solution to Priscilla's need, not just for girls to be with, but a school which would be more suitable, as the language and atmosphere in the boys' school was not right for her, and we felt a responsibility to take her out. It was her illness which brought a key to unlock the door to a marvellous answer. Dr. O. had finished giving her a diagnosis, and in writing out a prescription he began to talk about school.

"Why don't you put Priscilla in Monsieur F.'s school?" he inquired.

We laughed heartily, and replied, "Oh, Dr. O., we don't have that kind of money . . . even with a reduction we couldn't afford *that*!"

Later that week Monsieur F. and his secretary came for dinner and stayed for the evening. We talked about many things, and he thanked us for the time we were giving to the girls of his school. Yes, they were coming again, once a week, that winter too . . . and some of the girls had begged me to give them cooking lessons, so a morning of cooking school had been added to my list of things to do . . . with one Zoroasterist girl

48

from India delighting in her very first time in a kitchen.

"Why, I even had a servant to make mud pies for me when I was a little girl. . . . He iced them with a sort of plaster stuff, coloured. I *never* was allowed to do anything for myself."

Poor little rich girl! She delighted in the cooking but also in the wonder of all she was learning from the Bible, and, as you may imagine, the conversations in the kitchen were not all about recipes.

But to get back to that evening. Monsieur F. went on about his pleasure at what we had done for his school (without charge) and then said, without introduction, "And what would you like Priscilla to have? Just the regular American High School course—with advanced French with the French students of course—and will you want Latin?"

"But, Monsieur F., really there must be some mistake. We couldn't *possibly* put Priscilla in your school."

He brushed this aside and began talking about subjects again, but I pointed out firmly that it was all an impossibility. Then he turned to his secretary. "Mademoiselle . . . do we have food left over after meals?"

"*Oui*, Monsieur," she replied.

"And . . . *do* we have an extra bed?"

"*Oui*, Monsieur, in Shirley's room."

"Then," he said, turning to me triumphantly, "see? . . . it won't make the least bit of difference."

So it was that the impossible happened, and for the next two years Priscilla was a pupil in one of the best and most expensive boarding schools in Switzerland, virtually free of charge. We believe it was not "chance" or "luck", but a definite answer on the part of a personal God.

The wonderful part for the family was that through the winter months there needed to be no change. The extra bed was not needed, for Priscilla just went as a day student. She had ski lessons with the girls, emerging as one of the best skiers, in fact.

It was just at that point in our lives that we received a small-sized blow. Chalet des Frênes was for sale! The owner had come to Champéry preparatory to selling it, and she was not a "kindred spirit", in any sense of the word. She suddenly appeared one Saturday afternoon and swept through the house, selecting things from the walls, the cupboards, the drawers.

"I want this tablecloth, and I'll take all of this teaset today." (It happened to be the only teaset and had fifteen cups, badly needed for the next evening when the girls would be coming.)

"I don't think I'll take these dishes." (No, I didn't think so either, it happened that it was an antique set of cake plates Granny Fisher had given us in St. Louis. The idea!)

She was most difficult about every conceivable thing, and swept out saying, "You must let me know immediately, when I settle on a price, if you want to buy it."

We lived in comparative peace for a couple of weeks, borrowing teacups and later buying some new ones. Appraisers came to estimate the value of the house. Meantime more things were removed from under us. Finally the price came through. Fran and I opened the papers quietly before the fireplace. Our hearts fell. We knew we couldn't really buy it anyway, but this price was out of the question entirely. Good-bye, dear fireplace . . . good-bye house of dreams come true!

Susan came bursting through the front door in her news-telling manner . . . "Mother, Dad—"

"Susan, the price came—it is too much—we have to leave des Frênes."

"Will we? Oh, Mother, I have the most *exciting* news . . . I have been visiting at the V. home every day now, and Mme V. just said her four little girls can come to the class!"

In a few minutes the front doorbell rang and Susan and Debby raced each other to let Priscilla in. "Priscilla, guess what?" (We listened to see what the most important news would be.)

"The four little V. girls can come on Sundays—their mother said so. And our house is gone—we have to move."

House-hunting brought to us a "possibility". It was without modern conveniences, and had no resemblance to Chalet des Frênes. It was an old peasant chalet, which had mellowed and ripened through the years with changes and additions put in by artistic, imaginative people who had rented it for various periods of time. Chalet Bijou was the chalet where we had met Baroness von Dumreicher, and Chalet Bijou was to be our next home. It sat nestled down below the village, quite apart from other chalets, with a big field above it, between it and the village, a rushing torrent separating it from the path up to the village, and a wide field bordered by the torrent and trees . . . going down to a steep cliff that dropped to the river below, which ran out to lower valleys. There was a square balcony just outside the dining room, on the lower side of the chalet, which we called "the breakfast porch", because it had an old rough wooden table where we ate in the morning sun.

A field right next to us was sloped just at the right angle for practising ski turns, and the chalet had the cement, covered portion which is like an outdoor room with one side open, and has a stone water trough in it for rinsing clothing that has been boiled in a copper boiler (no—*we* didn't wash that way) and this closed-in, yet open, rough place made a perfect place to keep skis, which could be slipped on at any moment one had a spare half hour . . . and without expense or trouble, one was practising, and glorying in the beauty of the moment. The pale pink which changed to pale blue with the first bright evening star in it . . . was the most inspiring moment of the day to take a short "ski down two or three times" before eating supper. Oh yes, we had splintery floors; oh yes, we learned to heat with a granite stove which looked like a grave stone on one side of the living room; and to make fires in the "hole in the wall" which opened from the dining-room side. (The stove was without opening on the living-room side!) Oh yes, we grumbled about breaking ice in the early mornings when it had frozen in glasses in the bedrooms, and when it took hours to make any impression with a newly started fire, and hot-water bottles on the lap with blankets wound around us had to be the "heating system". It was far from perfect . . . but we learned to love it. It had a personality that couldn't be found in any modern "four walls and a ceiling" kind of room, or house *full* of such rooms.

The rent was much less than that of Chalet des Frênes, and

we immediately made plans to have hot water, make improvements in the bathroom, and gradually change it into a more comfortable place without removing any of the charm.

"Moving Day" could take a chapter by itself if this were just a humorous story. Hermann, the slightly "slow" but awfully good-natured brother of the two brothers and one sister who owned Bijou came with a big "luge" or sled, our only means of transporting our furniture.

Never will I forget the wild moment when I hung out of the window yelling, "What are you doing with that mattress?"

"We're putting it under the refrigerator."

"But I thought that mattress was already *in* Bijou and safely *on* Debby's bed?"

"Oh, yes"—they were being very patient with me—"We know that . . . didn't we just go all the way down there to get it?"

"But that is a *good* mattress, a special kind of one with little springs in it."

"Oh, yes"—still patiently—"We felt them, that's why we thought it would make a soft ride for the refrigerator!"

I soon had old quilts thrown out, and rescued the mattress for Debby. Happily we had found someone to help Hermann, because as far as I could see that day Hermann's part was confined to smiling from ear to ear and running downstairs two steps behind the man bearing a heavy load. . . .

The very next day was Debby's sixth birthday, and in the midst of trying to put away the most pressing things I stopped to make a birthday cake, jello, biscuits in the shape of chickens, and Susan managed the games for a party of village children and children from Home Eden. It seemed a "must" to have the party on the day itself, because we had to leave on the 6.17 train the next morning, Fran and I for Brussels (on a trip for the work), Debby for Lausanne where she was going to stay with "mama Turrian" during our absence, and Susan for *her* trip, across the fields to Home Eden, alone this time.

That was the way our time in Chalet Bijou began!

CHAPTER FIVE

Roots in Champéry

THE THING about real life is that important events don't announce themselves. Trumpets don't blow, drums don't beat to let you know you are going to meet the most important person you've ever met, or read the most important thing you are ever going to read, or have the most important conversation you are ever going to have, or spend the most important week you are ever going to spend. Usually something that is going to change your whole life is a memory before you can stop and be impressed about it. You don't usually have a chance to get excited about that sort of thing . . . ahead of time!

Betty and Gea were at the railroad station to meet us along with Susan, Debby and Marlise (a Swiss girl with us for some time) and Bob (a guest who had just "turned up"). We had heard from them and recognised them as the ones Baroness von Dumreicher had insisted that we must meet—"Dear Bettilie, you will love her." She had bored Betty stiff talking about us, but she hadn't really conveyed that we were so "wrapped up in Christianity". We weren't too overjoyed to have such a houseful . . . and Betty and Gea were pretty anxious to "get out of here" by the time they had gone through a couple of hymn sings and our usual reading of a Bible chapter after supper at night. It sounds dull, from both sides. But if there had been sound effects drums should have been impressively rolling in the background.

53

The girls had come for a bit of a rest after a motor scooter accident, and to satisfy the baroness. We felt we shouldn't say "no" to the letter, for the baroness' sake! They sunned themselves, went on walks, played the piano, listened politely to discussions about Christianity, and looked aloof most of the time. That is, they did for a week. Then Priscilla arrived for the weekend with friends from boarding school (girls bubbling over with questions because of their long talks with Priscilla). The girls were twins from London and Betty and Gea had to vacate because there weren't enough beds, but they wanted to come back Monday, and they'd stay at a *pension* over the weekend, they said.

Monday night they came, bringing a Jewish girl whom they had met. That night their real interest was kindled, and the conversation made the sparks fly. The following day after lunch they had so many questions, Fran decided we'd better make a fire so that they could be comfortable while he continued to give answers. The "answers" turned into a Bible study, and the rest of us crept out to give them an uninterrupted time huddled around the stove. I had a batch of rolls to knead and form as well as dishes to wash, but the rolls were all out of the oven in shining mounds and the dishes were finished . . . and still there was no sign of the concentration in the dining-room breaking up. With a basketful of orange rolls and cinnamon buns steaming and fragrant, and three cups of coffee on a tray, I walked into the dining-room to hear the eighth chapter of the Book of Romans being explained. That meant they'd already finished the first seven! My inner resentment that had been building up because of having to zoop around doing extra housework, while these girls sat around "resting" just melted at that moment. (If resentment can be said to melt!) It came from this sudden thought, "I'm sure God sent these girls here, whether they knew it or not!"

Betty's Swedish ancestry made her not only blonde but also quiet and reserved. She had a variety of interests, piloting a plane, music (she played an oboe and was studying at the conservatory of music at that time in Lausanne), travel and writing. Gea, who was with her in an apartment in Lausanne was dark and beautiful (Miss Wichita, Kansas, of the year before). She could both dance and play the piano and had Hollywood as her goal. Neither girl was expecting to find the Bible fascinatingly interesting. But suddenly a lot of pieces began to fall into place, and that night Betty said at the table, "I see it, I see it . . . it doesn't make sense if it isn't *all* true. It can't be taken in bits and pieces. Either it's all true or it's not." She didn't "believe it" at that moment, but she saw something.

The morning before they left, Betty came into the bedroom where I was making beds, and as quietly and calmly as if she had said "I'll take a dozen eggs" told me that she had come to believe the Bible, and wanted to "accept Christ as my Saviour right now so that the Holy Spirit will come into me, as you said He would, to help me to understand it as I read it."

As far as Betty is concerned, and Gea too (who wrote the same message in the guest-book, without saying anything to us) they will count that time in Chalet Bijou as a crisis in their lives. Betty you will hear about later in the story. As for Gea she today is the wife of a pastor in mid-west America, and the mother of five children. Her husband wouldn't be her husband, and the children wouldn't have been born, if it hadn't been for what happened that week in Bijou.

No, trumpets don't blow in life . . . as they would if we were putting on a play with sound effects. But we hear the faint echo in memory as we look back.

Speaking of sound effects . . . there should have been some very special ones one afternoon on the little train, as it came up from the valley below. But there was no music, no roll of drums, nothing to see or hear, as Mr. Ex. moved out of his seat and sat down by Fran.

"Excuse me, but you're a pastor, and I'd like to ask you some questions. You see I'm an agnostic, though I've been baptised a Roman Catholic . . . I'd just like to know what is the difference between the doctrine Catholic, and the doctrine Protestant?"

An earnest question but a simple enough one. Nothing earthshaking about the question. But the asking of the question, the answering of it, and the eventual effects in Mr. Ex.'s life, were going to result not only in a change that would have eternal results for him, but also in a tremendous upheaval for our whole family and our work. They were going to affect the lives of countless other people, too. *Some* sort of music should have accompanied that moment!

As it was, only the wheels of the cog railway kept clacking around as it groaned its way up the mountain, and Fran's voice competed with it as he explained some of the basic differences. He told him that historically the Bible is the Authority in the Protestant Church, as opposed to Rome's view that the Church is the supreme Authority. He told him of the fact that the Bible teaches that "salvation" is through faith in the "work" that Christ did when He died on the cross, and that the Roman Catholic Church teaches that "salvation" is a matter of faith plus works. Purgatory is a "work" of suffering, but the Bible does not teach of any purgatory.

A week later Fran stopped in to pay his electric bill. Mr. Ex. was not only the head of the Swiss ski school, but he headed the electric company in Champéry, and was active in its political life. (Champéry makes its own electricity, by the way.) The bill wasn't ready, so he said he'd come down one night and bring it. When he came his wife was with him, and as he and Fran talked in English, I talked to the wife in French. We had refreshments, and a thoroughly enjoyable evening. Before they left Mr. Ex. remarked, "You keep referring to the Bible. It is very confusing, isn't it? Who can understand the Bible?" Bibles were then brought out, and questions continued awhile longer, and he went home with a French Bible tucked under his arm.

Our next conversation together was in their home. During the week, Mr. Ex. had read Luke, John and half of Acts. He was disappointed that nothing had happened to him as he read, and that "lots of it means nothing to me". But he was full of questions. He went on reading, and asking questions for over a year and a half, and then one night as he sat in our living-room alone with Fran something very real *did* happen. What *happens* when someone "becomes a Christian"? Jesus said something about that to a very religious man named Nicodemus one time. Nicodemus believed God existed all right, and felt he was serving God in a very real way. But Jesus told Nicodemus that to be a child of God one has to be "born again".

I'm writing this by an open window, on Lake Geneva; the waves are wild today, and dry leaves are blowing in around me as I type. A weeping willow tree with green-gold autumn leaves still clinging to it is being whipped around like a girl's long hair in a speeding open car. What am I seeing . . . the wind? No, effects of the wind which make me know the wind is there. Jesus said . . . "so is every one that is born of the Spirit". What do these breathtaking words mean? They mean that Jesus is declaring that there is Someone who is called the Holy Spirit, who so affects the lives of the people He enters that results can be seen, which can be compared to the things our eyes see, the sensations our senses feel, when we are standing in the midst of wind. In another place in the New Testament we are told that at the very moment of birth—that is, this "new birth" Jesus was talking about—the Holy Spirit enters the person being "born". A Christian's life is dependent upon the reality of his having been born, and his having life . . . the life of the Spirit now within him.

What happened to Mr. Ex. that night was that he was "born again". Remember that I have only said "*what* happened", not *how* it happened. He had believed for quite a few weeks already that the Bible was truth, but now he had come to a place where he could step across a line, or into a circle.

There was a visible change in his life, but it wasn't hailed with cheers from his friends. His interests changed in that he preferred studying the Bible with a host of new books he invested in, rather than sitting around a café drinking. He didn't need the "escape". He had an assurance now that life did have a meaning and a purpose, and his thirst was for something very different. Does becoming a Christian ensure you a happy life? That depends on your definition of happiness. It certainly doesn't make you popular, nor understood . . . and it certainly *does* usher in a whole host of struggles and problems as you often stand alone in the family circle feeling quite uncomfortable. The deep, *real* joy that comes with knowing you are in contact with the living God is something no one would exchange who has known it. Becoming a Christian isn't changing your political party, or joining a new club, nor is it adding a sweet dessert to the hearty dinner of life. It is something that is so tough and hard in its reality, that if it were not *true* then it would be better to find a simpler solution to the problem of making this present life bearable. Talking about truth isn't very modern, but it does happen to matter a great deal whether there *is* such a thing as absolute truth, or not.

Mr. Ex.'s decision that night about the truth he was certain he had found was going to cause an upheaval in *our* lives that could not yet be foreseen.

During the summer of 1951, when Betty and Gea were with us, another Scandinavian trip was taken. The church services continued during the weeks we were in Champéry. Our gardens flourished and gave us vegetables for summer, and some to tin for winter. People came constantly to "ask questions". We wrote lessons.

Then winter rolled around again. Now rather than one boarding school coming for evenings, we had three coming three separate evenings, because each one felt too exclusive to let their girls mix with either of the other two! It was better that way, for conversation, but my arm nearly fell off making three big cakes (without an electric mixer or cake mixes) for each of the three evenings. When girls became really interested, they'd come alone for tea in the afternoon, or coffee in the mid-mornings, and one by one a number of them also became Christians. They kept in touch with us by correspondence. It was thrilling to see the evidence of the wind of the Spirit blowing in some of these lives.

Deirdre, an English girl, for instance, prayed aloud for the first time in her life when she sat with us beside that warm granite stove and said, "Oh God, I do believe that Jesus died for me. Please don't ever let me flinch."

She hasn't flinched either. She returned and went through four years of Art School, becoming the student vice-president and in all that time she continued steadfastly in her beliefs even though she was assailed with sarcasm and argumentation. Now she is working as an artist, but only until her husband finishes an engineering course. He is a Christian aviator.

Another "birth" in Chalet Bijou did make itself known ahead of time. I was expecting a baby and the three girls were taking the matter very seriously, as I had had one miscarriage, and they had no intentions of letting me have another one! "We want this baby," they said, and all their actions underlined the words. Susan made a poster headed with "What Expectant Mothers should Eat" listing the daily requirements in food and vitamins and illustrated with little drawings of fruit and vegetables. She hung it in a prominent place in the dining-room. If I sighed, or said, "oh" about anything, Debby would push me down on a couch and stick pillows under my feet. "Put your feet higher than your head. We don't want anything to happen to *our* baby!"

Their care of me had to be cut short during the sixth and seventh months, as we had to go to Spain and Portugal to speak, beginning children's classes there. My condition seemed to open the door very quickly for me to talk with Spanish and Portuguese mothers, so the only disadvantage was one of discomfort . . . a term doctors love to use for anything from downright seasickness to horrible pain! The children were overjoyed to see us when we returned, for more reasons than ever before: "mother is *still* all right," they gleefully welcomed.

Early the morning of August 3rd the wail of a newborn baby joined the wail of wind in the trees, as a summer thunder storm was going on, and Franky was added to the family. He was born at Chalet Bijou in our guest room—thereafter called "the hospital room". It had been hurriedly prepared by ousting the occupants in the middle of the night of August 1st!

Dr. Otten deserves all the human credit for our being alive, Franky and I, though I must say that for a time I didn't appreciate the doctor's humour. I was trying to follow *Natural Childbirth* from a book, and he kept asking me what page I was on! Perhaps if it hadn't been a complicated birth, the method would have worked. But it *was* complicated. Franky, who never has been still since, and has unlimited original ideas for getting into mischief, had started before he was born by getting himself into a very topsy-turvy position. Dr. Otten did a marvellous job with instruments, while the *sage-femme* gave me chloroform on a handkerchief, and Fran held a lamp. Priscilla's share was in squeezing orange juice for the doctor through the night. He preferred that to coffee.

The children delighted in the miracle of that baby being in his warm little bed next morning. I wish I had a photo of their three awestruck faces as they saw him for the first time. Susan always preceded her entrance into the room with the question, "Is he still there?" as if she expected someone to have spirited him away in her absence, while Debby just tiptoed in as if walking on eggs and never said a word. She just glowed silently!

Of course fitting a baby's schedule into the other work made an added complication, but during those early months he was an "easy baby" and when school hours were over he had three extra "mothers". We continued that winter to do all that had been commenced, using the quiet hours at night from eleven to two to do our writing when the girls from the schools had left, the household was asleep, and there was no danger of the phone ringing.

Before we went to the church for our Christmas Eve service (which had become a regular custom by that time), we made a strange procession across fields of deep crusted snow. Fran went first, carrying a tiny trimmed Christmas tree and a brief-case, then came Priscilla with a big box containing cake, bread, fruit, and Susan with another box of canned food. Debby behind them was empty handed, while I brought up the rear with a box that couldn't be tipped, as it contained a steaming casserole of scalloped potatoes, a hot roast of meat, a covered bowl of soup and some vegetables. Debby kept singing out "Look at me! look at me! I can walk on the crust . . . it doesn't break with me." There was just enough crust to keep the rest of us on top for a brief instant. Then we crashed through and had to bring a foot back up through its own "hole" or get stuck. We went down towards the little stream that tumbles into the rushing river. Fran put down his things to help us across.

Across more fields we went and down to the river, for the chalet we were heading for was perched on a sloping garden down there.

"How can that old lady, with only one good arm, ever garden here?" we asked each other.

We had heard that this old peasant widow had never had a good meal in her life, and we were on our way to see that she had at least one! For years she had lived in this lonely spot, after a miserable childhood and a life of hard work. We knocked, and an unkempt head appeared from a slowly opening door on the balcony—for the windows were shuttered tight to keep in any heat.

"*Oui?*"

A softening light came over the old wrinkled face. The door opened wider to let us into a room so dark we could see nothing for a few moments. Then gradually we could see the black smoke-covered walls, the piles of wood and the chopping block in the room's centre, the littered table with a half loaf of black bread and a small piece of dried cheese.

"We've come because it is the time of Jesus' birth. You know the Lord Jesus came into the world to take the punishment for those who would believe in Him." The children sang carols, we talked very simply to her. We lifted out the food—the steaming hot dishes, the tiny pumpkin pie and home-made rolls and cake.

"*Mais, mais, mais . . . c'est pour moi?* Am I to keep it? But I have never had such food in all my life . . . this is my *first* Christmas dinner." Now tears came into her eyes. Priscilla, who had been teaching in French for a long time now, gave her the Christmas story in French, and made as clear as possible that message which has "the answer".

After supper that night the children went by themselves to sing carols, and deliver boxes of home-made biscuits to various friends. There was Madame Fleischmann, the German widow who played our organ now, and lived alone in her tiny chalet. There were the Marclays, the teacher and the "puffy lady" at

Home Eden, the woman who rented us a piece of ground for a corn garden, and so on.

"I hope," declared Susan fervently that night, "I hope we can live in Champéry *for ever*."

Chalet Bijou Champéry

CHAPTER SIX

Return to Chalet Bijou

W HEN OUR mothers and friends who had come to New York to see us off became simply a part of the mass of backs moving quickly down the gangplank, we all tore up the nearest stairway to find a place at the rail where we could catch the last glimpse of familiar faces, wave and shout our final farewells. It wasn't until the whistle began its series of blasts that we discovered we were directly under it, and that the romantic, throaty voice of a ship's whistle announcing an arrival or departure was this time simply a fearful noise threatening to break our eardrums!

Once our baggage had been checked and found to be all on board, dining-room "sittings" signed for, and deck-chairs arranged for an inside deck where Franky could find no open rail, we sat down and began to compare notes with Betty. We had a lot to catch up on in her life, and she in ours, for we had arranged to meet on the ship, but it had been two years since we had been together in Chalet Bijou.

Betty and Gea had spent a year at a university together. Then Gea had married, and Betty had spent another year in a theological school, and had begun to write a regular newspaper column. Now she felt strongly that it was time to return to Switzerland for a period, to live at Chalet Bijou with us, learning what she could informally, and helping where she could as another member of the family.

We had lived through an increasingly busy winter after Franky's birth. Girls from the schools came three evenings a week, Priscilla taught a children's class once a week, others came for afternoons or evenings to bring their personal problems or spiritual questions (people from hotels, teachers or students), and we wrote our lessons for the scattered children's classes. Fran took a trip to Scandinavia alone, as I needed to care for the baby, and I also looked after the continuation of classes at the chalet. Then suddenly it was time to pull out trunks and begin packing to leave for America, for five years had flown past, and we were due for a furlough. The last weeks became an impossible rush of packing, yet we never wanted to turn away anyone who had special need of help. In the midst of it all Debby had her appendix out, as a reminder that life doesn't ever come in neat little packages of scheduled hours without interruption!

And now, after eighteen months in America—from May 1953 to September 1954—we were on our way back to Europe. It had been anything but a "rest" as we had both had speaking engagements taking us all over the country, and Fran had taught at a theological school, too.

We were going back with an expectation of something rather special, with an excitement to see what "God will do". We had done quite a lot of thinking and self-examining over the previous few years. It seemed to us that so much of Christianity was being spread by advertising designed to "put across" something, and that there was very little genuine recognition of the existence of the supernatural work of the Holy Spirit. One morning at Chalet Bijou's breakfast table, Fran had said to me, "Supposing we had awakened today to find everything concerning the Holy Spirit and prayer removed from the Bible—that is, not removed the way liberals would remove it, but that God had somehow really removed everything about prayer and the Holy Spirit from the Bible. What difference would it make *practically* between the way we worked yesterday and the way we would work today, and tomorrow? What difference would it make in the majority of Christians' practical work and plans? Aren't most plans laid out ahead of time? Isn't much work done by human talent, energy and clever ideas? Where does the supernatural power of God have a *real* place?"

Challenged by this, we began to think and look over our own lives and work . . . and, we asked God to give us something more *real* in our work of the future.

It was after supper during our last night on the ship, that Franky began to shriek and scream, "Tummy hurts, kiss it, tummy hurts, kiss it." He seemed to be in such violent pain that I wondered whether it might be appendicitis. Then he began to vomit, and this alternated with shrieking until suddenly he was relieved and fell to sleep exhausted in my arms. Of course the ship had a doctor, but at 11 p.m. on the last night at sea, with a sick baby that has just gone to sleep, and three other children ready for bed, one hesitates to call in a strange doctor. Sleep seemed the best medicine, especially when we thought it might be seasickness or a touch of intestinal 'flu. The morning came, with the urgency for repacking and preparing ourselves to disembark. Franky seemed better, and ate breakfast in his cot happily, though he had a fever and slept again until it was time to go out on deck.

Le Havre was flooded with brilliant sunlight as we approached the docks, and stood out like a study in buff, cream and tan against a bright blue backdrop of sky. When Franky, in my arms on the upper deck, wanted to get down and walk, it seemed a natural thing to let him run around a bit in the warm sunshine away from the crowd, before it came time to be lined up to await our turn to be checked through by customs and so forth. He was completely normal at that time, and as energetic as most healthy youngsters are even when they have a fever. It was the last time he ever walked without a handicap!

The open windows in the long narrow corridors of the boat train let in dirt and the clackety noise of the train wheels . . . but also bring the countryside almost into the train in a way that makes you feel you are walking through it all. However, darkness soon cut off our contact with the quiet fields, grazing cattle and lines of poplar trees of rural France. It was an exciting ride for all of us—the actual beginning of a new period of our lives—and a kind of home-coming at the same time. Franky settled down to sleep on my lap.

As we arrived at the Paris station, Fran began handing our bags out of the window to a waiting porter, and I wrapped Franky carefully in a blanket so that he wouldn't get chilled as we walked to the hotel nearby.

"A good night's sleep, and a day in bed tomorrow, and he'll probably be fine for the rest of the trip," I said.

Franky looked around him and said solemnly, "This is Paris, Mommy, this is Paris," with the air of making a great discovery.

The next morning Fran, the girls, and Betty went out sightseeing, and to have tea with a French pastor. Franky was still asleep, and I left the dark curtains drawn across the windows, sitting quietly beside him until late afternoon, when he stirred. I stepped to the window to pull back the heavy drapes and a streak of sunlight streamed across the floor. In this path of light Franky was stumbling: Franky who had walked with perfect balance on his two sturdy legs since he had been nine months old. His legs seemed to be sticking strangely out from the hips until he went down in a heap!

"I can't walk, Mommy . . . I *can't* walk!" he wailed, with a question in his voice.

"Oh, Lord," I prayed. "Can it be *that*? Oh, if it is, please give us wisdom to know what to do."

I gathered him up in my arms and tried to be calm for his sake. "Let's string some beads, Franky," and we began some quiet games on the big bed. I couldn't leave him to go anywhere. We were in a little hotel room down near a Paris station. It was nearly four-thirty in the afternoon, and we had train reservations to leave early the next morning! When Fran and the girls burst in I had to let them see what happened when Franky tried to walk. This time it was worse. Doctors differ so. We preferred not to get into the hands of the wrong one at that moment.

"Let's call Doctor O. in Switzerland, and get his advice." Several hours went by without success. No answer.

Fran then called the airport. "If they have places on the morning plane, you, Franky and Debby will go by plane tomorrow. That will give you only one hour of travel instead of ten hours."

There were just the right number of places left, so it seemed this was the right step to take. Calling "La Maison de la Bible" in Paris, we discovered that the Christian *sage-femme* (midwife) I had had when Franky was born, Helen, was visiting there, and would be glad to come and help me to get to the airport with the two children. Again we did not feel this was "chance", but an added indication that it was the right thing to go on to Switzerland by plane.

At Geneva the warm sun took away any chance of chilling, and Franky awakened to talk so brightly that our friend Mr. B. who had met us felt he couldn't be very ill. We drove past peaceful, sleepy-looking villages and terraced vineyards, along the blue lake sparkling with a dancing brilliance in the sun. "Could anything really be wrong?" It seemed like a figment of my imagination. We stopped once to telephone Dr. O. and there was still no answer, so Mr. B. drove on until we reached Aigle. Again we telephoned, and, giving up, decided to call our old doctor in Lausanne. She gave us the name of someone to see in Aigle.

After a thorough examination, including chest X-rays and testing of knee reflexes the verdict was given, "Just a little touch of *grippe* and fatigue."

I wanted to believe this, but I knew it was not correct.

"But doctor, what about the fact that he cannot walk?"

"A touch of rickets, give him these."

So I went off with Franky, and a bottle of medicine for rickets, to find that the rest had arrived by train in Aigle, and Mr. B. was offering to take us up to Champéry. It was getting dark by that time, and everyone needed to go to bed early.

It was not a very gay homecoming, though nothing could dampen the girls' ardour at the first sight of Champéry. "Oh, doesn't it *look* good? Doesn't the air *smell* good? Isn't it *home*?"

The next morning another doctor was recommended—a

67

Monthey surgeon who had made a special study of polio ever since his son died with it years before. Our call brought him up in a short time, and his examination brought the immediate pronouncement: "You son has polio, and the present effect is in the lower back muscles and the left leg."

He ordered hour-long hot baths, and massage, and said he would come again soon. A three-minute phone call to a doctor friend in America, Dr. Kiesewetter, head of a children's hospital, brought a comforting piece of advice—to go ahead and care for Franky with the hot bath treatments at home, but to keep him very quiet for a couple of weeks, too.

That phone call was a remarkable thing. The connection came through clearly, I related the symptoms for a minute and a half, and then the line was cut dead. The operator was "so sorry", and said she would get the call back as soon as possible. Fifteen minutes went by. In America the doctor used that fifteen minutes to call a polio expert in his hospital, using another phone. He got the expert consultation he wanted, and when he came back on the line to Switzerland, was able to give advice based on that consultation. Chance? I don't think so. We had prayed that God would use that call to give us the assurance we needed concerning Franky's treatment. The next few days found us living among half unpacked suitcases as I spent all my waking hours caring for Franky, and that included some of the night hours as he frequently awoke screaming. He was too young for us to explain what was wrong, and with our knowing as little as we did about polio, it was not until later that we discovered these were spells of muscle spasms—and very painful. It is awful to awake with a sick feeling in the pit of your stomach as the memory suddenly floods back with, "Oh yes . . . I remember what's wrong." This was my first feeling each time I would awaken from the sleep that erased emotion for a time.

Fran had to go to Southern Italy to speak at a conference of missionaries. We had been planning to go together, with Betty staying with the children, but of course I did not leave. It was while he was away that Franky had his second attack, which is said to be common in polio. The Monthey doctor sped up the hill, arriving at night, to beg me to let him use the injection which he had discovered for polio. He insisted that Franky was already beginning to show signs of paralysis on the right side, and that his invention would be the only hope of stopping it. It had only been used on six human beings before, but he himself was certain of its effectiveness.

"Please let me use it. Don't deny the boy the possibility of this help. He may never walk again otherwise."

Here it was, almost midnight. I was alone in the decision. My tongue clung to the roof of my mouth with the fright that had dried up my saliva. An injection which would put Franky in a state of shock. An injection that would need to be done under ether. Hadn't I read somewhere that all injections are dangerous during polio?

The doctor walked up and down the bedroom on the creaking wide boards saying, "Hurry, hurry, there is no time to lose, its effectiveness depends upon doing it early enough."

The doctor's daughter whispered in my ear. "Papa really feels this is the right thing to do."

I felt I was going to be sick. How could I *know* what to do? Supposing he died under the ether? I cried out to God silently, "Oh, show me what to do, God. Oh Father, show what is best for Franky. I'll go with the doctor, unless you stop me, God. I don't know how else to do it."

The decision was made. I don't believe I was alone in it. Was I flooded with calm confidence? I was not! I sat on the back seat of the car, feeling constantly more sick as Franky chattered so happily about the fog below us looking like the ocean. We came into the quiet, small hospital. The ether mask was put over a face growing red with screaming and fright, and I was led out of the operating room into the hall.

I knelt by him all that night, praying, watching and listening. Each time he would awaken his first word was "Juice", and I'd pop a bottle of strained orange juice into his mouth. He'd suck a little and go off to sleep. The doctor had said he was going to give him a second treatment in the morning. I became increasingly frightened about it. But in the early morning as I was reading my Bible, there beside Franky, a verse in the Book of Proverbs suddenly hit me. It was this: "The king's heart is in the hand of the Lord, as the rivers of water: he turneth it whithersoever he will." That is what "hit me". I thought, "If God can turn a King's heart the way He can turn the course of a river, surely God can turn the decision of this doctor in the direction that will be best for Franky"; and as I asked God to do this, I felt comforted and stopped trembling.

The doctor walked in with a nurse a few minutes after that, and as she started to pull the cot towards the door, to take it to the operation room, the doctor put up his hand and said rather sharply, "Wait". Then he silently gazed at Franky for a few minutes and finally said, "I've changed my mind. We won't do it." The second injection was never given.

We spent a week in the hospital, Franky and I. I nursed him, rather than having the French-speaking nuns do it. Betty meanwhile held the fort at the chalet, being a tremendous comfort to the three girls as well as doing practical work.

At the same time, Fran was in Pescara, Italy. After one of the conference sessions there he received a long-distance telephone call from Priscilla to say that I was in the hospital with Franky. She told him that Franky had had the second attack and asked him to come home. That night he caught the midnight train from Pescara. It took from midnight until twilight the next day, by train, to reach the hospital where Franky was. He said that it was a time of real revolution in his own heart as he began the journey, thinking of Franky and what it could mean. However, as the long hours dragged by he wrestled with the problem of trusting the Lord in the real things of life and by the time he could see the hospital in the distance he had come to a place of trusting even in this. This was no small battle and in a certain way this personal struggle and its result was also a part of the base which God was laying for the work which was ahead.

Whatever that injection did, Franky did *not* have any paralysis on his right side, and the day came when he could sit up, then stand, and finally walk. That winter the baths and massage treatments continued, and a little tricycle was bought for him to use for exercises. His indomitable will forced him to keep trying, for after that first wail over not walking, he never mentioned it again, but just *determined* to pick himself up and go on no matter how many times he fell.

To go ahead with the story of Franky, just let me say that what he finally was left with was a zero muscle in the calf of his left leg, and muscles which measure three inches in the front of his left leg (four inches is perfect). He has had to have a brace, has had to go through a muscle transplant, has had many frustrating things to face in the function of his leg. It hasn't been easy for him to take, or for us, but through it all there have been a tremendous number of instances of answered prayer, and results which even Franky in his bitterest moments has recognised as good results which have come out of the tragedy.

In spite of the handicap, Franky is now able to ice skate, and he is in his school's hockey team and soccer team. He has won the silver medal in ski-ing; he can swim, even quite long distances. All the rest of his body is that of an athlete.

But this is to anticipate the story. Our first autumn back in Switzerland—the time we had looked forward to so expectantly —began with a case of polio to nurse for long weeks.

A scene in Huémoz

CHAPTER SEVEN

The Clouds thicken

T HE DARK cloud of Franky's polio was added to by layer after layer of other clouds. One bright October day Susan came in from playing tennis after school, and complained, "I think I've turned my ankle, it hurts and it's kind of swollen." A day or two later Susan had been hiking, and complained again, "I must have twisted my knee . . . it hurts so much, and it's kind of red and swollen."

Dr. O.'s face looked grave after he examined her. "I'm sorry to tell you this, as it seems you have enough on your hands, but Susan has rheumatic fever and will need to be in bed for at least two months!"

We remembered the severe case of infected throat Susan had had in America in the spring, realising that the background had been there for this. The "two months" was going to turn into the greater part of three years . . . in and out of bed!

A letter was written to Calvert Correspondence School, and the eighth grade course ordered for Susan; a wooden shelf was built outside her window to serve as a bird feeder and give her the fun of bird-watching from her bed, and her bed care was added to the schedule of baths and massage and exercise for Franky. Debby crossed the fields alone those months, as the only one leaving the house for school. Priscilla, who had graduated from Steven's School in Philadelphia the year before, was ready for college, but had decided to study alone until spring, cramming French and other subjects preparatory to entering the University of Lausanne. When Betty had to leave in November, it was Priscilla who "filled in" as part-time nurse.

Chalet Bijou wasn't just a hospital during that time, however. The living-room was constantly a scene of teas and evening discussions, as well as of lesson writing. Classes and church services continued, but there was a heaviness from foreboding clouds hovering over it all.

We hadn't yet received our *permis de séjour*. A permit must be obtained every six months, by strangers living in Switzerland (after the first three months of tourist time is over), and we had always had ours without delay. A trip had been planned to Finland, but the combination of our not having permits, plus the illness of the children, caused that to be cancelled. We decided to use the time "saved" by making the changes we had planned in the chalet "since we'll be living here for the next ten years at least".

Rumours drifted to us of trouble concerning our permits because of Mr. Ex. and the children's class, but others in the village who had heard the rumours shook their heads and said the equivalent of "pooh . . . nothing to it".

The next word we had came from Sion, the Cantonal centre of the government. It was a summons for Fran to appear at one of the offices at the *Bureau des Etrangers* there. Priscilla went along to be sure everything would be understood by both sides as far as language went, and one of the village men said he would try to be a help. However, he had to stay outside the dark little office during the time of questioning. He had quite a wait, as the questioning went on for two full hours! A big dossier was opened where records of everything we had done during our time in Switzerland seemed to be contained. Questions were asked as to our church services, the children's class in French, the Bible classes, the purpose of our trips to other countries, whether we ever did any speaking on politics, whether we were acceptable to other Protestants, why we had given biscuits and hot chocolate to children in the class, and so on. As far as Fran could tell, the man seemed to have a favourable reaction to the answers, and said he would try to get a five-year permit for us so that we would not be bothered in the future, but to just "keep quiet about the questioning" and wait for the permit to arrive.

There was a nasty, nagging worry that kept coming into our minds concerning that "five-year permit" . . . especially when we paid the bill for upholstering the furniture—furniture which belonged to the chalet, not to us—and as we brought in electric lines, put in a hot water system, painted, relaid floors, and so on, all at considerable expense.

It was during this time that Fran had thought of the name *L'Abri* (simply French for "The Shelter") as a name that would be good for our chalet, as we envisaged its work in the future. We looked back over the years in Champéry, and realised that although we had not gone there for that reason, we had had a constantly increasing number of young people, and others, coming to us for spiritual help.

"Let's call it *L'Abri*, and let these people know that they are welcome to come back and bring friends with them."

We pictured girls from the schools, coming back in later years, to stay at hotels or *pensions*, and to ski or hike during a few weeks of vacation, interspersed with afternoons or evenings of Bible study and discussion at Chalet Bijou or *L'Abri*. When we felt most "down" during the piling up of difficulties, I made a folder telling what *L'Abri* was going to be, naming *pensions* and hotels where people could stay, if they wanted to come to us for spiritual help.

Then those avalanches and floods descended suddenly upon us . . . and all else was forgotten for some days. All that is, except the immediate needs of a family from India, staying at a hotel, whom we went to see some evenings, because they could not get to our chalet through the rubble.

One day, after the soldiers had left the village, and danger of more avalanches had ceased, I was sitting at my typewriter, feeling that "haunting question mark" along with the heaviness that went with the uncertainties ahead for the two sick children and a combination of problems that seemed to deluge us. I propped my Bible up on the keys of the typewriter, and asked God to give me the help and comfort I needed. My reading took me into the beginning of the Book of Isaiah. (Not because I opened the book haphazardly, but because that was the next portion, as I read straight through.) Now I believe the Bible is, to the spiritual life of a Christian, what warm fresh whole wheat bread is to the physical life—both nourishing and appetising! There are also times when God speaks to some of His children in the very words of the Bible, written hundreds of years ago . . . yet seemingly written as a message for the situation of the moment.

What do I mean, "God speaks"? Does one hear a voice? I personally never have. I simply mean it in the sense one uses it concerning other printed words "speaking" to one with a special message.

Let me tell you what happened that day. I read this: "And it shall come to pass in the last days, that the mountain of the Lord's house shall be established in the top of the mountains, and shall be exalted above the hills; and all nations shall flow unto it. And many people shall go and say, Come ye, and let us go up to the mountain of the Lord, to the house of the God of Jacob; and he will teach us of his ways, and we will walk in his paths" (Isaiah 2:2).

My feeling was one of excitement. I read it over again, and then again . . . then reached for my pencil and wrote in the margin: "Jan. '55, promise . . . Yes, *L'Abri*". For I had had the tremendous surge of assurance that although this had another basic meaning, it was being used by God to tell me something. I did not feel that "all nations" were literally going to come to our home for help, but I did feel that it spoke of people from many different nations coming to a house that *God* would establish for the purpose of making "His ways" known to them. I felt these people would tell others, and would say in effect, "Come . . . let us go up the mountain . . . to the house of the God of Jacob; and *He* will teach us of His ways, and we will walk in His paths". It seemed to me that God was putting His hand on my shoulder in a very real way and that He was saying that there would be a work which would be His work, not ours, which man could not stop. I felt that this work was going to be *L'Abri*.

That was a moment of excitement, tying in with our feeling when we first started back across the ocean—the feeling that God was going to do something, as we wanted Him literally to take over our lives, and use us as He wanted to, not according to our own plans.

Did I then have a calm that nothing could disturb? Did I go on with an unruffled peace? Not at all. In fact, although I had said, "Oh Heavenly Father, we want *Thy* plan, not our own; we want definite assurance that *Thou* art leading," I went ahead with my unmanageable vivid imagination, and planned the sort of thing *I* thought *L'Abri* was going to be— and that plan all centred in Chalet Bijou, Champéry, and a beautiful tucked-away grassy place which was like an out-door amphitheatre, where I pictured gatherings of fifty sitting on the grass for an outdoor service. Oh no, I didn't stop having ideas and imaginations!

Now you have enough background to step into the kitchen with us on February 14th, and to feel something of the emotions on the reading of those two pieces of paper which gave us six weeks' notice to leave!

Out? Out of Chalet Bijou?

But this is our home . . . we haven't any other.

Out of Champéry? Our work is here: the church services, the three girls' schools coming right now, and the boys' school added to that this very winter.

What about our dream of *L'Abri* and the people planning to come even that winter to ski, and to be near us? Out of *Switzerland*? Where would we go? What money would we use? What about our furniture?

Out in *six weeks*? . . . but Susan and Franky weren't in any condition to travel.

Dismay, incredulity, a trapped feeling: "Impossible"—is a word that was going to be constantly in our minds through coming days.

We all drifted into the living-room together to sit down as a family—with one addition, Eileen. Eileen is an English girl, an agnostic, who was with us at that time. She had "run out of money" and had wandered down the path one day asking whether she could help out in some way, "for board and room", so that she could stay on and ski a while longer, before going back to London. She skied in the afternoons, and the rest of the day she helped in innumerable ways, entertaining Franky and Susan with hilarious stories from her experiences as a travel guide, and making herself a welcome member of the family. Now, deeply shocked by the news, she followed us into the living-room to see what we would do next.

Fran said to us, as we sat in stunned silence following our first outburst, "As I see it, there are two courses of action open to us. We could hurry to send telegrams to Christian organisations, our Senator in Washington, and so on, trying to get all the human help we could possibly get; or we could simply get down on our knees, and ask God to help us. We have said that we want to have a greater reality of the supernatural power of God in our lives and in our work. It seems to me that we are being given an opportunity right now to demonstrate God's power. Do we believe God is *able* to do something in government offices, in this present situation, as He was able in times past? Do we believe our God is the God of Daniel? If so, we have an opportunity to prove it now."

We chose to pray, rather than telegraph frantically for help, and we knelt down as a family, with our one curious onlooker, and we prayed, each one out loud, one at a time, right down to little Franky. "Dear Heavenly Father, please show us what to do." "Oh God, let us stay if it be Thy will." "Dear Lord, guide us."

When we got up from our knees, Fran said, "While we were praying it occurred to me that we ought to let at least one Swiss Protestant friend know immediately what has happened. It seems to me that that is imperative, before any rumours start going around. I'll call Mr. A. in Lausanne right now."

Mr. A.'s reaction to the reading over the phone of those two papers gave us a key as to what the reaction of almost every Swiss person would be. Mr. A. is our friend, and he knows us well, yet this is what he said, "I'm sorry, and I trust you . . . but it seems to me there must be a mistake in your understanding of the words. Perhaps your French is not accurate enough. You see, I just don't believe it. It couldn't happen in Switzerland. I tell you what you must do. Send one of the children down to me with these two papers *immediately*, so that I can read them for myself."

We dispatched Susan with a brief-case and the papers, on the first train, to be met with Mr. A.'s car, and cared for lovingly at their home that night so that the trip would not be too much effort for her.

With Susan on her way, things began to buzz at the chalet. There were letters to write to our families letting them know the plight we were in, a phone call to make to the Marclays who came immediately to see us, and to weep over the "edict". "This can't happen. It isn't religious freedom, and we are supposed to have liberty," was their reaction.

A bit of supper was hurriedly prepared and eaten—the Valentine supper now a forgotten thing, and the special cake added to the other cake for the boys in the evening. Mr. Ex. came down to tell us that he felt sick over what had happened, and to say that some of the men in the village intended to get up a petition to have the edict changed so that we could stay. "They don't realise the power of the Church. If the Bishop had said you must go, even a liberty-loving lawyer would fold up—the pressure is too great."

Fran and I left on the early train for Lausanne the next morning. A call from Mr. A. had told us that he saw the papers were just as we had said. But he added that the fine print at the bottom said, "You have ten days to appeal." The date was written in with ink and only thirty-six hours of that ten-day period now remained. "Come to Lausanne tomorrow morning," he said, "the Chief of the *Bureau des Etrangers* has written a proper appeal for you, both to Sion and Berne, but you must come and sign it immediately."

When it was signed it was sent off to the two offices by express delivery and registered mail and arrived just within the date allowed. So the possibility of the appeal being thrown out because of a technical reason was thwarted. . . . We felt this to be an answer to prayer.

We had lunch with the A.'s, during which time both Monsieur

and Madame kept insisting that this "couldn't be done in Switzerland". The afternoon found us in Geneva, visiting the American Consulate, to "report that we had been put out of the country". When one lives in a foreign land, one is obliged to report any such thing to the consulate! The Consul kindly gave us an hour and a half of his time, but his conclusion was: "America has no treaty arrangement with Switzerland whereby they are obliged to keep any of our citizens here. Hence, America could not help you in any way officially. However, I want you to report this to our Consul of the Embassy in Berne, and I urge you to go to Berne to see him immediately."

He called someone in an office somewhere else, in the same building, and in a short time we were handed a list of trains to Berne, both for that night and early morning, plus a letter of introduction to the Consul of the Embassy.

We had been invited to the *Ecole Biblique* in Geneva for supper and the night, so decided on a 6 a.m. train. Mr. Alexander and our Swiss friends at the Bible school were shattered at the news for a time, but their reaction was to have a prayer meeting with us, and the time of spontaneous prayer was a tremendous experience of the reality of a unity among Christians, when it is as it should be.

The next morning it was dark and cold as we drove off to the station at 5.30 a.m., and a hymn that Mr. Alexander had written kept pounding through my head. The hymn speaks of how Christ was accused by men, rejected by man . . . and goes on to speak of how Christians are *with* Him, also rejected.

As the train started I felt chilly and depressed in the pit of my tummy. Hot tea and rolls in the dining car didn't seem to help in the least, and we went back to our wooden-seated coach to settle down to our usual private Bible reading.

I had been reading one chapter a day in Isaiah since that day when I read the second chapter (then I read from the New Testament and the Psalms—a sort of "balanced diet" of reading). Now on the train that sixteenth of February, I read chapter 30. How can I be sure? . . . Well, it's all marked up with underlinings, and the date! I'll just give you a few of the phrases that were underlined as I read on that morning train: "One thousand shall flee at the rebuke of one; at the rebuke of five shall ye flee; till ye be left as a beacon upon the top of a mountain; . . . and therefore will the Lord wait, that he may be gracious unto you . . . blessed are all they that wait for him . . . thou shalt weep no more; he will be very gracious unto thee at the voice of thy cry, when he shall hear it, he will answer thee. . . . And thine ears shall hear a word behind thee, saying, This is the way, walk ye in it, when ye turn to the right hand, and when ye turn to the left . . . Ye shall have a song as in the night when a holy solemnity is kept; and gladness of heart . . ." As I read, the cold, sick, depressed feeling left me, and I was filled with a warmth of expectancy and faith that God *was* going to guide us, and that He *could* do the impossible and that He *would* show us the "way". I felt a great surge of thankfulness to Him for giving us an opportunity to really *see* Him work, and I prayed, "Oh Heavenly Father . . . please show us *today* something of Thy power. Give us a sign of the fact that Thou art hearing us as we pray concerning this whole thing."

I arrived at Berne with a feeling of confidence and joy. Fran had also found assurance in his reading in another portion of the Bible. And so we shared our feeling of assurance that something good was going to happen that morning as we walked through the fine snow which sprayed our faces with tingling, multiple stings and waited for the Embassy to open.

CHAPTER EIGHT

Can God work Details together?

WE WERE shown into the office of the younger Consul, who quite evidently had, as a part of his task, the shielding of the senior Consul from being bothered with unimportant things. His attitude was one of polite superiority, as he listened to our story, and assured us that there was little any American could do about it.

"You see," he said, "Switzerland is one of the few countries which have no treaty agreement to cover this sort of thing with the U.S. and their law is such that they reserve the right to eject anyone they want to without giving any explanation. The *cantons* are supreme and each *canton* may do what it wishes to about keeping or ejecting foreigners. It *is* strange that this has been made to apply to all of Switzerland, but as for the Canton of Valais, nothing could be said about their decision. Why don't you just go somewhere in another country —like France?"

We had come this distance only on the insistence of the Consul in Geneva. We had a letter of introduction to the senior Consul (one step in rank immediately below the Ambassador). Respecting the letter of introduction the Consul reluctantly said, "I'll give you ten minutes with the senior Consul." We followed him up a staircase, feeling more than ever like outcasts.

The Consul rose and greeted us, then took the letter and

began to read. "Oh!"—turning to Fran—"I see you were born in Philadelphia. So was I."

"What part of Philadelphia?"

"Germantown."

"So was I."

"What school did you go to?"

"Germantown High School," replied the Consul.

"Why, so did I," answered Fran, "What year did you graduate?"

"A long time ago now. In fact it was 1930."

Fran's face broke into smiles of recognition as he exclaimed, "Why, that was my class too!"

The Consul looked again at the name in the letter and said, "Why, *Francis Schaeffer!*" slapping him on the back and pumping his hand heartily.

"*Roy Melburne . . .* of all things."

"Francis was the Secretary of our class. I went to school several years with him . . . think of it!" said Roy, turning to the now astonished younger Consul. "Twenty-five years since we met. Tell me, Fran, what you've been doing all these years? I've been all over the world myself. Just got into Switzerland a few months ago."

And so they launched into a conversation about mutual acquaintances, old times, and their lives since then. . . .

Finally the Consul asked, "Now what is all this about?" As can be imagined, Roy Melburne was ready to open a sympathetic ear to our case. The story was retold, giving us an opportunity to speak of things which are basic to us, concerned with that which we believe to be truth, which gave added purpose to our coming to Berne. Roy listened with interest. He then gave us an office in which to write letters for the rest of the morning while he worked, so that we could go home with him for lunch, for early in the conversation he had excused himself, phoned his wife, and said, "I'm bringing an old school friend home for lunch, dear, with his wife."

After lunch he arranged an interview for us with the Ambassador. Madame the Ambassador, Miss Willis, was very gracious as she received us in her beautiful office, and exclaimed over the coincidence of two friends meeting at such a time. She too heard the story of what had happened, and expressed amazement. But the fact that no American could officially do anything to help was clear.

However, she said, "I'm going to a cocktail party tonight, and I'll just happen to mention to the Chief of the *Bureau des Etrangers* that it is strange that one of the Consul's old school-friends is being put out of Switzerland." Roy Melburne said he would also ask some questions about the matter.

We believed all this to be an answer to prayer, on the part of a God who exists, and who listens to His children when they pray.

Did this incident at the Consul's settle the matter? Not at all. But it was one shaft of sunlight coming through the clouds. It was, to us, a sign that God had heard our prayer and that He had reminded us of His power to work in ways beyond our imaginations. It was an encouragement for that moment, but it was something more important—it was a definite thing to look back to, when the way seemed hard . . . a "marker" behind one on a path is a comfort until the next clear mark is found.

We got back to Lausanne in time to attend to some business before the 6.30 p.m. closing hour. In the travel agent's, Monsieur B. was incensed when he heard what had happened. "I'm going to call my good friend the Chief of the *Bureau des Etrangers* here in Vaud."

A few minutes later, as we were mailing the letters we had written in Berne, in the Lausanne Post Office, we bumped into Mr. F. the director of the girls' school Priscilla had attended. He was disgusted and shocked at the news and said, "I'm going to call my good friend the Chief of the *Bureau des Etrangers* here in Vaud." This was the same man to whom Mr. A. had shown the two papers the day before. So three of his "good friends" were speaking to *M. le Chef* within a very short number of hours.

This Chief sent word to us that there was only one way we could make an appeal. He was sending us a sheaf of pale green forms to fill out. However, the forms required something that could not simply be written in. We were told that we had to find a house, in the Canton of Vaud, and apply to live *in that house*. The name of a particular house had to be placed on those forms, and it could only be one which we had definitely arranged to live in. Because we had to have a village or commune agree that they wanted us in their location, and then they would have to ask the officials at the head of such matters in the *canton*, then the *canton* would have to make an appeal to Berne to have the edict annulled. There was no other way to make an appeal.

What an impossibility that seemed to be! Where would we find a house? Where should we look? Why would a village want to be bothered helping with this appeal? Many were the discouraging questions that filled our minds as the cog railway car creaked and groaned its way up the mountainside in the dark that night. We found Priscilla was beginning to wear down a bit under the strain of having the full responsibility for the care of the younger children and the home. The phone had been ringing a lot, and she was beginning to get reactions from the village. All sorts of reports and stories were buzzing around. The one which upset Priscilla the most was a false report that we had already been "kicked out" of Lausanne! A fresh supply of food, easy to prepare, from Lausanne shops, and the story of what had happened in Berne, cheered all the children. The telling of that story was to us that night the same as taking a backward glance at the last signpost. It seemed that we must take the *next* step of looking for a house.

The next morning we started off in a blinding blizzard, in our ski clothes, to get the early morning train. We were house-hunting in a country where we had been given notice to leave! It was a strange feeling. We had looked over a map and had decided in which direction we would go. It was at this point that my memory of that verse in Isaiah fitted in. We talked of our dreams of our chalet being a shelter—*L'Abri*—for students or others in the mountains for ski-ing. It seemed that Bijou had been ideal, but if there were to be a change, surely it would be another mountain place? Money and time were both factors in our choosing to look in the closest ski resort in the

Canton of Vaud—closest to Champéry, that is. That place was Villars.

We walked down the central street of Villars looking around us with curiosity. How many schools came here, we wondered? Would there be an opening for a chapel service such as we had had in Champéry? As we made some inquiries at the *Bureau de Tourisme*, we were told that an Englishwoman who owned a hotel could tell us what we wanted to know. Soon after that we were sitting in the lovely living-room of her hotel, with big felt slippers (kept at the entrance for that very purpose) over our ski boots to protect the Persian rugs. Sipping tea, we were telling our story up to that point, and asking for advice in looking for a chalet.

She insisted that we come back for the night, had a porter come and take our small suitcase to a double room, and told us that at whatever time we were through that way we were simply to go into the big dining-room, and a cold supper would be waiting for us, so that we need not come in time for the dinner hour, and thereby waste any precious time. Chance? Luck? Let me say I have never had another hotelkeeper do such a thing for us, as a *gift* to complete strangers. To us it was a gift from a personal God who understood that we would need strengthening, and not only with food and a place to sleep.

Soon we were wading waist-deep in snow to look at chalets to rent. There were only a few possibilities on the list, and we discovered that the rent for the very smallest of summer chalets, much too small for our family, would be *double* the rent we paid for Chalet Bijou. This, we began to realise, was a much more expensive resort. We made our way to other nearby places—Arveyes, Chesières, and then Gryon, following every "lead" anyone gave us. By the time we finally trudged back along the main road and over a bridge into Villars again, it was late at night, and there had been nothing but things which underlined the word *impossible*. That cold meal was not only waiting, but a waitress had been told to add hot soup and tea to it when we arrived! A bedside lamp spread a welcoming light over those two fresh-looking beds with the covers turned back. It was a comforting thought that Jesus had said in the New Testament that even a cup of cold water given in His name would not be forgotten by Him.

The next morning brought the same disappointments, and we went back to Chalet Bijou for the weekend, feeling as though we had come up against a brick wall.

We returned to find that a Christian businessman had stopped to visit us. Having him for dinner, after our church service, drinking coffee and eating home-made ice-cream together—made it seem like a normal Sunday and the nightmare aspect went away for a few hours. Two unlooked-for helps arrived during that weekend. The businessman left an envelope with a cheque "to help in these next days", and the phone rang, bringing us the voice of a friend in Lausanne who said he had arranged for a lawyer to organise certain things concerning our case, such as the petition some villagers were signing on our behalf. But there were those sheafs of green paper, and not an encouraging hint of any "name of a house" that could complete those forms.

"We'll look for two more days and if we find nothing, we'll have to give up the search."

This time our first moments in Villars brought us face to face with Professor C. and his wife. "Could you have tea with us, and help us with a problem in our lives?"

Our own urgency of finding a chalet seemed a greater need, at first, but Fran whispered to me, "If they need us, we can take an hour," and we agreed, glancing at our watches.

The C.'s had had a very tragic past. Professor C. was a Czechoslovakian displaced person, who had escaped into Switzerland barefooted after having been in a slave labour camp. His wife was a Swiss whose parents had deserted her when she was fourteen to go into Germany during the Hitler régime, and she had not heard from them again. We had come to know them through an unusual incident.

It began one winter day when Priscilla was chewing her pencil in frustration over second-year algebra which she was studying alone, in preparation for our going back to America and her entering third year high school in Stevens. "I *can't* do it," she cried, "nobody could. I can't do second-year algebra without a teacher."

"But Priscilla," we said to her, "Have you prayed about it?" We were thinking that God could clarify her immediate problem, so that she could get past the barrier that was making her feel desperate.

"Oh, I've prayed about my studies in general, but not particularly about algebra," was her reply. That night we all prayed for special help from the Lord for Priscilla's algebra.

The following day the telephone rang. The voice was heavily accented: "I am a professor in a boys' school, and I have been coming to your church services, with my wife. My wife, she has need of spiritual help. Could you talk to her?"

We arranged for them to come for tea. When they came, it was discovered that the wife did not understand English, so Priscilla translated for her the next two hours—her questions into English, and Fran's answers into French. As seven o'clock came they hastily rose to their feet and said they must go back to supervise the boys at supper, but they asked wistfully if they could return. We assured them they could come back after supper to finish the conversation. That night Priscilla's translation went on until 1 a.m., at which time Madame C. suddenly said, "Oh, I do *see* . . ." meaning that she understood and believed. A few more questions brought her to the place of wanting to pray, to thank God for what He had done for her in the death of Christ.

And a half-hour later her husband was praying in much the same manner . . . "I've looked and looked for an *answer* to life, now it is clear to me. Oh, thank you so much." Then he turned to Priscilla. "Mademoiselle Priscilla, what can I do for you? You have made all this possible for my wife. Otherwise she could not understand."

"For me? Oh, nothing, I've been *glad* to translate for you," said Priscilla.

"But I am professor of mathematics—can I not help you with *some*thing?"

You can guess Priscilla's exclamation of surprise as she almost screamed, "Oh Mommy, my *al* . . . gebra!"

88

Within moments Professor C. had taken her book, made a quick outline, and had told her he would be glad to tutor her twice a week to help her get through the allotted amount in the next couple of months. When he came to give her a lesson, Madame C. always came along and asked to help with mending, ironing, or anything she could do. Not only was Priscilla prepared to enter her class that spring in Chestnut Hill, but my preparations were also helped in a way that I could not have visualised.

Now to return to our unexpected meeting with them in Villars: we were standing with a slight bit of hesitation in the lobby of a boarding school where we had met, a place where Mr. C. was making a decision concerning his future. Before we left the building to find a tea-room, Madame C. whispered agitatedly into my ear, and with alarm I led her aside to get a further explanation. She was seven months advanced in a pregnancy, and the information she frantically conveyed was enough to make me rush to the headmistress of the school.

"Excuse me, but Madame C. is in need of a place to lie down, immediately, with feet higher than her head . . . and I need to use the telephone right away. I feel it is an emergency."

I called her doctor in Lausanne. He told me to keep her lying down, and to call Dr. Méan. I called him and he came immediately. He said the baby would be born sometime that night, in his opinion, and told me to call a taxi and make arrangements for the hospital. The following couple of hours melted away between phone calls, and the preparations needed to make the back seat of a taxi into a make-shift ambulance. Finally at five o'clock all was in readiness and Madame C. was tucked in in the taxi with pillows, blankets, sheets, towels . . . and I was rather nervously standing with one foot in and out of the taxi. Then the doctor said, "Now, Madame Schaeffer, you sit right there . . ."

Me? *I* must go? But what about our house-hunting? What about our precious time that was melting away like ice-cream on a radiator! "But, doctor . . ."

"Yes, Madame, you sit there, as of course you *have* to go with her. There is no one else. Her husband must sit in the front seat . . . he is worse than useless right now, the state he is in. You *must* go."

It seemed final and there was really no decision to make. The taxi began moving slowly down the mountainside, as though driving on glass . . . and I waved to my dismayed husband, and began a trip that was to make me feel like Alice in Wonderland. It just didn't seem real. The taxi driver seemed to feel that his business in life was to go as slowly as a car would go, without coming to a dead stop. It took three hours to do a trip which usually takes an hour and twenty minutes! And my night was spent with Madame C., as having no other "family" she clung to me in a way I could not reject.

The baby was born at four the next morning, and as Madame C. was rolled back into her room, I followed to sit in a wicker chaise-longue for what was left of the night . . . dozing a few minutes in between praying for God's help in our finding a chalet "in time to fill in those forms—oh *please* God."

The baby weighed less than four pounds, and lived only two weeks. The C.'s have never had another child. It was a moment when they needed someone to be "family", and even during that night I was thankful I had been able to help supply that need in this crisis in their lives. I knew that it was not chance that we had met them that day.

When it was time to leave the hospital and hurry down the hill to the Lausanne station, my mind was rapidly calculating how many hours there would be left to house-hunt. It was lunch time by the time I arrived in Villars, going the long way through Bex, and I telephoned Champéry to find out how things were going there. Fran had decided that the lost day was really the "final straw" as far as any possibility of finding a chalet in time went, and was in the throes of packing books, some to store, some to take with us if we were going to have to leave the country.

"But if I find a chalet on my own today, will you come back with me tomorrow and look at it?" I asked.

"Yes, if you do . . . though I doubt if you will," he replied.

This fired me with determination to find something, and I started out with the feeling, "I *will* find something. I will." Yes, I prayed, but with a sense of almost demanding, with a lack of humility, and a feeling of spiritual pride that I had not given up and had faith enough to keep on. Oh, I didn't analyse this at the moment, I just ploughed through the snow with my flow of adrenalin carrying me on in spite of having had no sleep. I determined to do it without even the help of real estate men . . . I *would* find something.

I don't know what I expected, but I felt that I'd find just the right place by looking, literally, at all the chalets in the area. I must say that looking at houses with people in them made me feel like a lost child gazing wistfully at other children safe in their homes . . . and I was very close to tears.

Suddenly I saw a "for rent" sign on a weatherbeaten looking rustic chalet, very large, but a possibility. I inquired as to the whereabouts of the owner, and walked on, another mile and a half, to a school in Arveyes, where the owner was head-mistress.

This very dignified lady quoted the price and then went on to say something about a grand piano, antiques, Persian rugs . . . but the price had blurred the rest out, and I burst into tears. The price for *one* month was what we had paid for a year in Chalet Bijou.

I dabbed at my eyes with my handkerchief, trying to explain my lack of control.

"Oh, excuse me, I don't usually break down like this. But you see I had no sleep last night. Assisting at the birth of a baby. Now I have to find a chalet . . . (I looked at my watch) . . . within an hour, or we'll be put out of Switzerland."

She looked at me with a pitying look, and I read in her eyes what I felt to be her judgement, "This person is a little off her head . . . better ease her out of here." What she actually said was, "I am sure you need a cup of tea, my dear . . . but if you'll excuse me, I'm teaching a French class right now . . ." And before I knew it I had been gently propelled to the front door, and I was on the outside!

Feeling I had made an utter fool of myself, I went slowly

down her path, and on into deeper snow. There was no place to turn. Suddenly I began to pray.

"Oh, Heavenly Father, forgive me for my insistence on my own will today. I really do want to want Your will. Please help me to be sincere in this. Forgive me for closing the door in my own attitude toward the possibility of Your having a totally different plan for the next step of our lives. Oh God, I am willing to live in city slums, if it is Your will."

Suddenly, in the midst of my prayer, I felt a surge of faith in the God of Elijah, Daniel and Joseph. I prayed: "But God, if You want us to stay in Switzerland, if Your word to me concerning *L'Abri* means our being in these mountains, then I know You are able to find a house, and lead me to it in the *next half hour. Nothing* is impossible to You. But You will have to do it. I can't even talk to anyone without breaking down."

I went down towards the main street of Villars just as a chattering, laughing crowd was coming back from ski-ing, crowding into the tea-rooms.

The steps leading to Chalet les Mélèzes

CHAPTER NINE

A Personal God
. . . A Specific Answer

ALKING THROUGH the lighthearted crowd I kept my eyes down on the snowy pavement, not even looking up to beware of the skis which might poke me, as they bounced along on the shoulders of the skiers hurrying to get something hot to drink. I felt my eyes might be showing signs of my having been weeping, and I didn't want to see anyone.

Suddenly I heard my name. *"Madame Schaeffer, avez-vous trouvé quelque chose?"*

And I looked up to see Monsieur G., a real estate dealer, to whom we had talked several days before. He had not shown us one chalet even, as he said everything he had was "de luxe" and far above the price range we had mentioned. I was surprised that he had even remembered my name.

I answered, *"Non, Monsieur G. . . . rien."*

His reply to that was to step over to his car, open the door and say, "Hop in, I think I have something that might interest you." He drove off, stopping to make a couple of calls and then beyond Villars down the mountainside. "Would you mind living in Huémoz?" he questioned.

"Huémoz, where's that?" I asked.

And he waved his hand in the general direction we were going, saying, "Oh, down there."

We drove on down the mountainside for a few minutes . . .

fog blotting out the view, and weariness blotting out any enthusiasm on my part. The car came to stop right beside a Postal Bus stop sign, and a mail box. We climbed out and went up a pair of log steps, buried in the snow, and opening a gate made our way through unbroken snow to a door opening from a step, level with the ground at the front of the chalet. I looked up at a big chalet, tightly shuttered, with full length balconies on the two floors above, and then walked into a musty dark room, while Monsieur G. opened shutters letting in light, and explained that it had not been lived in, except by holiday-makers, for a long time. We went over the chalet together: three floors, made into three apartments; small kitchens, no living-room for teas and discussions—but a big place, really, and suitable. There I was, within the half-hour, not because I had had wisdom or cleverness to find it, but because God had answered my prayer. This I believed to be the only explanation.

I arranged with Mr. G. to meet him the next morning with my husband. As I watched him turn the car to start back up to Villars, something occurred to me.

"Oh Mr. G., I forgot to ask . . . how much is the *rent*?"

"Oh it's not for rent," he replied, "it's for sale" . . . and then the car shot forward on up the road.

"For sale," I repeated to myself dully. "For sale! We have no money, and even if we were millionaires, who would buy a house in a country without having a permit to live there?"

This seemed the last straw to me for a few moments. I was feeling sick with exhaustion by this time anyway, both from sleeplessness and the emotional struggle. Then as I rode down on the bus, and up on the train, I began to review the last days, and the last hours of that particular day. It seemed to me that the "markers" or "signposts" of answered prayer, indicated very definitely that God had been leading up to *this* point. Surely He would not lead to a dead end, and the next step on this path was to return and look at this place the next day. Before I arrived back at Chalet Bijou I was convinced that God had given me a clear sign and that I must go back the next day to that chalet to which *He* had taken me that afternoon.

When I arrived home it was to discuss the most recent news they had received. "Berne has given us an extension of time. That is we may stay in Switzerland until the matter has been studied, but Sion has sent word that they will give *no* extension of time, and we have to be out of this chalet and this village and this *canton* by midnight March 31st. Franky's doctor even telephoned Sion to tell them that the children should not be moved at this time, for health reasons, but no extension was given, unless we and the children would sign a paper saying that we would not talk about religious matters to people in or outside of our chalet!"

Also that evening a phone call came from the lawyer in Lausanne who was collecting the fine letters villagers were writing on our behalf, and the petition, and so on, to say "You must hurry to find a house, as those papers *must* be filed within a day or two now."

Both these pieces of news underlined my certainty that the next step was to go back to look together at Chalet les Mélèzes in Huémoz. I described the chalet to Fran, told him it had twelve rooms and supposedly a marvellous panoramic view, but I did not tell him it was for sale. I was frankly afraid he would say it would be no use even wasting the time and car fare to look at a house for sale!

That night I prayed again, fervently communicating my fears and uncertainties as to my own honesty in wanting God's will, as well as concerning the situation. One can't put an hour of talking to God in a paragraph, but it is important for you to know that it was an hour, and not a sentence; and that there is a two-way communication in prayer, and the reality of the Holy Spirit's work in a Christian during the actual time of praying. As I asked for God's guidance concerning the chalet which had seemed such an exciting answer to prayer that afternoon and now seemed so impossible, my own logical sequence of thought brought me to begin a sentence in which I expected to ask that the owner change his mind and let it. It was after a length of time during which I had been inwardly struggling for reality in my sincerity of wanting God's will, when I came to this specific request concerning the chalet. It was then that suddenly I became flooded with a surge of assurance that God can do anything, nothing is impossible to Him. My sentence changed in the middle, and I ended my prayer with a definite plea, which even startled me as I asked it, "Oh, please show us Thy will about this house tomorrow, and if we are to *buy* it, send us a sign that will be clear enough to convince Fran as well as me, send us one thousand dollars before ten o'clock tomorrow morning."

The following morning as we went through new layers of fresh snow to the train, the postman—his packages and mailbag on a sled—handed us three letters. We opened these on the train, as the morning sun suddenly slipped over the rim of the mountains and poured light and warmth over the light wooden seats. One was from Paris, the next from Belgium . . . and the third was from a man and his wife in the United States. Mr. and Mrs. Salisbury had been following our work with interest and prayer, for quite some time, ever since they had been spiritually helped through Fran's messages in a conference they had attended. However, they had never given financial help to our work in any way, nor were they wealthy. They knew that we had been told to leave Switzerland, and had been following the story up to that point. It was Mrs. Salisbury who wrote the letter:

"I have a story to tell you that will interest you," she began. "Three months ago Art came home from work with an unexpected amount of money. The company had decided to pay the insurance premiums for all their employees, and this was made retroactive for those who had worked there a certain number of years. Art's amount was a great surprise to us. We decided at first to buy a new car, then came to the conclusion that we didn't need a new car. Our next thought was to invest in buying a little house, which we would rent. We went to look at houses, and as we looked over a very likely small house I suddenly saw signs of termites in the beams. 'Look, Art,' I said, 'Doesn't that remind you of the verse in Matthew which says, Lay not up for yourselves treasures upon earth, where moth and rust doth corrupt, and where thieves break through and steal: but lay up for yourselves treasures in heaven, where neither moth nor rust doth corrupt, and where thieves do not break through nor steal.' I then asked, 'Art, would you be willing to take this money and invest it literally in heaven? . . . rather than investing it in another house on earth for added income? Would you be willing to give it to the Lord's work somewhere?' He replied, 'Yes, Helen, I would.'

"Well . . . that was three months ago, and all during these three months we have been asking God to show us what He would have us do with this money. Two or three times we almost gave it to some cause, and each time we felt stopped from doing it. Now tonight we have come to a definite decision, and both of us feel certain that we are meant to send you this money . . . to buy a house somewhere that will always be open to young people."

The amount of money was exactly one thousand dollars!

You can imagine that my tongue was suddenly loosed, and I poured forth the story of both my prayers, and the fact that the house was for sale. As the train arrived at Ollon, and we stepped on to the yellow bus . . . both of us were convinced that God was leading us to buy Chalet les Mélèzes.

Later we discovered that Helen had been ready for bed when she finished writing that letter, and suggested to Art that he mail it on the way to work the next morning. However he felt such a strong urge to mail it that night, that as she got up from her knees where she was praying by her bedside, Art said, "We must mail it now," and getting out the car, they drove through a blinding rain storm to the main post office to mail the letter right then. The perfection of the timing of its arrival, the *timing* of both my certainty at the moment I prayed, and his certainty of the need of mailing the letter were amazing. Then her statement that it was for buying a house, "that would always be open to young people" was almost a prophecy of our future work. Neither she, nor we could have known at the time what an accurate prophecy it was.

Chance? Coincidence? Luck? To us it was a tremendous instance of answered prayer, a wonderful demonstration of the existence of a Personal God who deals with His children as individual, meaningful personalities, and in an individual way.

We stepped off the bus at that bus-stop which was to become the familiar place of arrival and departure for such a variety of people in coming years. That morning it was a deserted place, with an empty house above it, and another enormous empty house at one side. Again a fog formed a wall to hide the view. Mr. G. had opened the shutters and we were soon looking through the chalet with curiosity to see what God had chosen for us, not with the feeling that we were making a choice at all.

"Yes, we'll take it." It was easy to say that that morning, with excitement and assurance that we had had an unmistakable sign from God that this was to be our answer. We were in high spirits, and no obstacle seemed very important at that moment. When he told us that we needed to get a 10,000 dollar mortgage, and would have to have 7,000 dollars cash, we didn't even bat an eyelash . . . not *that* morning. We were in a hurry to get away, fill in the sheets of paper, and send off our appeal to the right offices.

We took the first bus back down the hill, to connect with a train to Lausanne, and went to see the lawyer, the police and the notary, to be told that we had found the chalet just in time, another day would have been too late! The Chief helped us to fill in the papers properly, and he told us that they must first be sent to the President of Ollon (in which "commune" Huémoz was situated). When we saw his name, Fran remembered that he had already met him, and that he was a friend of Mr. Ex.'s. It was Mr. Ex. then who himself presented these papers to the commune's president, with explanations!

A few days later Mr. A.'s uncle telephoned us from Lausanne, saying "I understand you have decided to buy a chalet. I want to say that it is a very risky thing to buy a house in a foreign country where you know very little about property. I am a notary, and real estate is one of the things I care for in my work. I would like to offer to go and see this chalet you are arranging to buy, and let you know what I think of it, as a property."

My reaction was one of fear, I must admit, as I thought, "What if he says it is a poor buy . . . what then? Haven't we been guided to buy it?"

Fran replied that he felt it was an opportunity to ask God for another sign, trusting God to make the way clear to us. "Let's pray that if it is right for us to go on with these arrangements, he will find it a good buy."

That night when I heard Mr. D.'s voice coming through the phone receiver, I didn't want to hear his reply, I so feared it might be the wrong one! Then his deep voice brought these words into my consciousness, with a flood of relief: "Madame Schaeffer, this is the *best* buy I have seen for a *long* time. However, someone else is really almost ready to buy it, and you must put the 'Promissory Payment' on it tomorrow. That will be 8,000 francs. Do you have enough money?"

I put my hand over the mouthpiece of the phone, and said, "Oh, Fran, how much money do we have? A promissory payment has to be put on it tomorrow."

Now there was a little pile on a desk in our office, with a paper clip on it . . . a little pile of letters that had had gifts in them. There was the money which that businessman had left, the thousand dollars, and then some other gifts.

One example will show you why we felt that the timing of these gifts was not mere coincidence. Christian, from Norway, who had visited us in Champéry years before, had never written to tell us why he had not returned to the University of Lausanne, although we had sent him news from time to time. During that week a long letter came, telling of the tragedy which had changed all his plans and which had interrupted his education for three years. Now as the way had opened up to him to continue his education in Scotland, he said he wanted to let us know what had taken place. He went on to say, "I hear you have been put out of Switzerland. I want to pray for you, but I want to do more than pray. When I was in Lausanne I had some money in the bank. Now I am sending word to the bank to send it to you. I want you to buy a door with it which will always be open to fellows like myself. . . ." A door? at what other point in our lives would this have made sense? Both his letter and the Salisburys' contained a prophecy of our future work which has had more meaning as time has gone on.

Fran quickly counted up the various amounts that had come

to us in a variety of ways—each person having been led to send an amount they felt strongly they should send. The total came to *exactly* 8,011 francs.

"Yes, Monsieur D.," I replied, "we have enough money!"

Arrangements were made to make the promissory payment the following day, and very binding papers were signed. We promised to make the payment on the house on May 31st! They promised to let us move in and live there, "rent free", for the months of April and May, until that final "down payment" and mortgage were combined to give the owners the full amount.

We had given 8,000 francs (about 2,000 dollars) and had said we would give another 5,000 dollars by May 31st or forfeit all that had been given, plus a lot more. This is the rigid and binding agreement of a promissory payment. It was a frightening thing to sign. The wonder of having just the right amount of money, and the further guidance of Mr. D.'s judgement as to the "good buy", made it possible to sign the papers and hand over the money with great confidence. It was later that the enormity of what had been done hit us. But gradually the trail markers, or signposts *behind* us, were increasing.

The chapel fireplace

CHAPTER TEN

A Personal God
. . . His Interest in Detail

THE NEXT few short weeks of March were a jumble of "in betweens"! In between packing, we stopped to talk to village people who came one by one to find out what had happened. In between talking to village people we prepared regular meals. In between cooking meals we took care of Franky's special treatments. In between Franky's treatments we dismantled the rooms, taking down curtains, books out of the bookcases, and so on. In between clearing the house we answered innumerable phone calls, often bringing us new "impossibilities". In between phone calls we prepared refreshments and kept the living-room presentable for the groups continuing to come three evenings a week from the schools. In between the coming of school groups we wrote countless letters, in reply to the deluge of mail we were getting.

There were regular services in the chapel, kept up till the last Sunday. There was the C.s' baby's funeral in Lausanne. There were requests for lessons and illustrations for children's classes to wrap up and send off. Our regular life and work had not come to a standstill to wait for us to catch up with it. This is the amazing factor in any time of upheaval in anyone's life. There is never a neat little portion of time labelled: "Time for exclusive care of upheaval, all other obligations have ceased." Food had to be prepared, dishes washed, clothes washed, teeth brushed! And though the search for "truth" and "meaning" is something many people intend to take time for "some day", there is no neat little portion of time that will drop into your lap labelled: "Full stop ahead for contemplation and search for meaning in the universe." The end of life just comes up and hits you while you're not looking!

In the midst of all this, we were told by the lawyer in Lausanne that we must not plan to move into Chalet les Mélèzes to await the decision concerning our permit! We must wait in a "neutral place", which he defined as a hotel in some other *canton*! This made all the packing a great uncertainty for a few days. Were we packing to go straight into another chalet, or were we packing to store half the stuff and take suitcases to a "neutral place"? You can imagine the increased feeling of living in a bad dream that this piece of information gave us.

It was two days before the moving date, or "ejection date", that we received an answer to this prayer. "You may go ahead and move to your new chalet, and wait there for the final word."

This answer had come through Mr. Buchser in Lausanne talking to a chief in Berne, and his subsequent talking to various men involved, and getting the permission made official. From a human viewpoint it could have gone in either direction.

The night when representatives from a "moving firm" came to look over the things to go, could easily have been filmed for a comedy! They even *looked* like Laurel and Hardy. A tall, thin man and a short, stout man walked around peering at things in a most unbusiness-like fashion, making irrelevant remarks, and asking questions that sounded more as though they were considering putting things in a museum, than moving them to another chalet for us.

They put their fingers under things, like the refrigerator, the stove, a box of books, a trunk, without ever budging them, as if to weigh them—one finger under, then a wise nod of the head! The girls were in fits of giggles before they left. When they came to the studied conclusion that they could move us, the date was settled upon (March 31st!) and they promised to come at seven in the morning.

Two days before the moving day, the phone rang again,

and it was the moving company. "So sorry, but we can't possibly move you . . . not now anyhow. We forgot about the avalanches. Your road is gutted out, the bridge won't hold, the fields are nothing but mud in this present thaw . . . so we can't move you."

"But we *have* to move. We can't choose another date . . ." Nothing that we could say changed their conclusion. They could not move us, and that was that.

Eileen had become accustomed to having us all assemble in the living-room after some new problem arose, and followed us in again this time. It was only moments after we had gathered to thank God for the solution concerning *where* we were to go on the 31st! Now . . . *how* were we to go? Again we each prayed. Before we had finished the phone rang again.

It was Mr. Buchser, of the Kuoni Travel Agency. "How is everything going, Madame Schaeffer? Are you ready to move?"

"Oh, Monsieur Buchser," I replied, "we have a new problem, the moving company say they cannot move us because of the conditions of the roads and paths after the avalanches. We don't know what to do about it."

"I have a friend, Mr. Schneider, who is just starting a new moving company. I'll call him. He is really a versatile fellow. He'll have an idea."

Mr. Schneider came that evening with his young son, and a big dog. He looked over the chalet's contents rapidly and efficiently, making notes. As he stood by Franky tucked into his cot for the night, he started a conversation with him which was another answer to prayer, a very "gentle" one for the need of a very small person.

Franky had been terribly upset by the barrels of shredded paper being gradually filled with our dishes, as I packed a few at a time in between other things, and even more upset by the taking down of his curtains, pictures and bookshelves.

"Say, Franky boy," Mr. Schneider said, "Do you like jeeps?"

Franky's brown eyes got bigger and darker than usual as he answered, "Oh yes, I *love* jeeps."

"How would you like to ride in mine?" Again those brown eyes widened with excitement and assent.

"Well, I've thought of a plan to get these things of your family's over to Huémoz. The roads down to this chalet can't be used, but I have a Land-Rover jeep, and that can cross anything. I'll take the things by jeep, across the fields, and up to my truck which will have to be left up on the village street. The jeep will have to make many trips across the fields, and you can sit on the front seat and help me!"

From that moment on Franky looked forward to the moving. This might be called coincidence, chance, or luck . . . but I felt that it was a very special detail on the part of an Infinite Person who has limitless variety as well as power in caring for the tiniest details.

After a week of rain, moving day dawned with a partially clear sky and not a drop of rain fell all day. Two trips were made by the stubby little jeep carrying boxes and furniture across the bumpy fields to the truck on the road above, before the men stopped for their breakfast of coffee, bread, butter, cheese and jelly, served in an assortment of left over dishes and glasses spread out on a table in the middle of the living-room—a kind of ludicrous "finale" to the entertaining that had taken place in that room!

The four puffing men, with the addition of Hermann, Fran and Norbert Marclay, carried things out to the jeep all morning long, and the jeep went back and forth, back and forth with dogged determination to do away with the obstacles the avalanches had placed in the way! Franky was the blissful front-seat guest for each trip the jeep made, and he took on a new swagger with the importance of his position, leaning against a wall, crossing his feet, to drink a glass of milk in perfect imitation of the workmen drinking coffee! The first truck load left before noon, to go to Huémoz—Fran, Norbert, Debby, Franky and a couple of the men filling up the jeep as it followed close behind. The top of the jeep was down, and they waved to people on the village street and the ones who were "for" us waved energetically back.

Susan had already gone to Huémoz the day before, with

Madame Fleischmann, who insisted on going to help make beds, and have something ready there for our arrival. Susan overdid it however, and ended up with a new attack and hence started her time in Chalet les Mélèzes back in bed!

That left Eileen, Priscilla, Rachel (one of the owners of Chalet Bijou) and me to go on with the last-minute packing and clearing up, making a few last phone calls and visits before the jeep and truck came to prepare the second load. Dark had come before we were finally ready to leave, and this time the jeep had its top up to keep us a bit warmer on the drive. As we passed the chalet of our "egg woman" she ran out to say good-bye with tear-filled eyes. Then we came to Rachel's chalet, and she ran out with a little bag of night-clothing for she had offered to come with us for a few days to help, sacrificing her precious working time, as well as courageously riding off with us as we left a few hours before the deadline of our eviction. Crossing the Rhône river in the valley below a half hour later we were out of Valais, and in Vaud. Our being "put out" became a physical reality. It was a strange emotion to have, looking back across the river, to realise that it had not been our choice, and that at that time we could *not* go back if we had wanted to!

We awakened the next morning, 1st April, 1955, to see our "view" for the first time. What a view God had chosen for us! It was a tremendous thrill to look out at all we had been given without choosing. Just before, or just after a time of much rain, there often comes a day as that one, with the air so clear that everything seems magnified. We set a small wooden table that stood out on a square balcony at the corner of the middle floor, with a blue and white tablecloth and put blue and white Dutch plates, cups and saucers on it, and all the food for breakfast. There we sat in the warm sun to "drink in" the view, along with the tea!

We could look right across the Rhône Valley, counting fourteen villages and towns hugging the mountainsides, or dotted on one side or another of the Rhône river below. Looking up and beyond the inhabited parts of the mountainside, we could see the rocky, snow-covered tops of the Dents du Midi (our old friends!), a gleaming, glistening glacier, and many, many other peaks. Keeping our eyes at the upper peak level we could see jagged snow-covered granite peaks mingling together, in the soft blue sky, with fleecy puffs of white clouds on three sides of us. Behind the chalet we saw there were no peaks, but steep grassy fields that disappeared in thick, dark pine woods. Just below the front hedge bordering the lawn there was a twenty-foot drop to the road, so that when the morning bus stopped, we could only see its roof from the breakfast table. That bus connects with the train, and from Aigle a person can go straight on to Lausanne, Geneva, and on to London, Paris, etc., directly . . . or if going in the other direction the train in Aigle also goes straight to Milan, and points south! We marvelled that morning that rather than a mile long struggle to a station, we now had transportation directly from the foot of our front steps! We marvelled because it would be so easy for us, not knowing that this perfect location as far as transportation goes, was also to be useful for many, many visitors who would be coming!

We had "Family Prayers" after breakfast (which consists of reading something from the Bible, praying, and at times also singing a hymn). Our family consisted of the six of us, plus Madame Fleischmann, Rachel, and Eileen. It meant that without our realising it, *L'Abri* had started with our first meal in Chalet les Mélèzes, with a German musician, a Swiss peasant, an English ex-Wren and ex-nurse and travel guide, for our first guests!

The two rooms on the ground floor were bedrooms, each with a washbasin, a pot-bellied stove, a bed, a hanging light with a velvet moth-eaten fringe around it, and bedraggled "lace" curtains tied back at each window! The movers had added trunks and boxes to fill up these two rooms. By dint of much hard work Fran had cleared out all the boxes, trunks, beds and other furniture from one of those rooms, had found twelve straight chairs and placed them in three rows, had found a table to place in front of them, had discovered an old wooden screen in the attic, and had placed it around the old rusted washbasin. And presto!—he had a place ready for a church service. So our first Sunday there we had a service, with our three guests and the family, and Mr. Ex. who came for that hour. Rachel left sobbing that night, not knowing when she could see us again. Madame Fleischmann left the next morning.

Eileen had expected to leave on the eight o'clock bus Monday morning, but she and I sat up until the wee hours of the morning talking, so she put off going until later. Her agnosticism had taken a different form as she said, "I just tingle up and down my spine at all the wonderful things in the Bible we study at Family Prayers. I always thought Christians were dull, unhappy people, but you all seem to be so excited about it . . . and your life has been anything but dull! Heaven and eternal life sound so real when you tell about them, and I think 'why don't I jump to accept?' And then something holds me back. I can feel a struggle going on inside me which I don't really understand. You see, I am not desperate about anything. I like life as it is and I haven't been unhappy or felt a need, and well, I guess I like my independence. I don't want someone else's will instead of my own. I keep thinking, if I accept this, perhaps God will want me to go off to the heart of Africa like that Doris who was here last week. And I wouldn't want to be without enough water!"

Eileen wrote back from England later: "I'm finding it hard to settle down, and for the first time in my life I'm not enjoying London. I am reading my Bible, but most unmethodically— usually in the midst of doing something else—unpacking or cooking, and when something is about to burn. I also have had long discussions with various friends during which I propound your views with great fervour and little knowledge and then suddenly wonder which side I'm on anyway!"

We were all very fond of Eileen. She is someone we still hope to see "accept"—as she hasn't, not yet.

But to go back to that week in April. Now we were alone: no telephone, no electrical equipment (Huémoz had 130 voltage at that time, everything we had was 220 volts—so we didn't even have an iron we could plug in), no help, everything packed or "hidden", it seemed; and suddenly we began to feel the tremendous hindrance to even daily living, let alone work, that this being put out of home and village was going to be. And we had no word concerning our permit.

Easter weekend Priscilla went to Geneva to attend a Bible conference, and the rest of us stayed in the chalet, as Debby had had an injury from a bicycle spill, Susan was "dragging" around, and Franky had had enough changes for a while. The stimulation of having had a place to go on the day we had to leave had diminished, and a heaviness came over us as we thought of the young people in schools in Champéry whom we could not have for tea, and of whoever might be in the chapel waiting for an Easter service. After our little Easter service in the drab old bedroom, brightened up a bit with daffodils Mr. Marclay had brought to us, we went for a walk along one of the paths that was later to become so familiar to us all, wondering whether we *really* were going to live here!

An added depressant came in the form of food poisoning we all had on Monday, evidently coming from cream-filled pastries that had been substituted for my usual home-made cake. Susan was so violently ill she begged me to promise to send her eyes to a New York hospital (the address of which she carefully gave me) when she died! . . . so that the cornea could be given to someone waiting for one!

Tuesday Fran decided that in spite of feeling "seasick" he would go on to Lausanne and meet Priscilla to help her enrol in the university, and as he was there he decided to go on in to visit Mr. R. at the police department. Here he discovered that our entire permit affair had been placed in the hands of the Committee of Education and Religion, and that they were the ones who were to make a recommendation to the police department concerning our case! More complications! The department never would have telephoned to tell us this, but with Fran there in person, they advised us to go to meet the president of a committee dealing with the affair. An appointment was made for the next Saturday afternoon, and then Fran bumped into Mr. A., unexpectedly, who insisted that someone accompany us on Saturday to help explain the matter to the president.

109

A coincidence? A very carefully *timed* one we felt, especially as we later saw the importance of each of these details fitting together.

Meantime I had had a letter from Madame Fleischmann, answering the question we had had in our minds as to what had happened in the little chapel, our first Easter Sunday of being "out". She said she had awakened with a feeling of urgency: "I must go to the little church and play the organ and pray for the Schaeffers."

She got dressed, sat and studied the Bible study in German we had given her on the resurrection, then felt "now it is *time*"—with a strong sense of duty—and picking up her Bible, the study, a hymnbook, she hurried off down her steep little path in the direction of the church in order to be "on time". Alone in the church she went into the little side room we used "in between seasons" and lit the two electric stoves and sat down to play hymns. Suddenly the door opened and people began to enter . . . people, and more people until there were forty! They were English visitors from hotels, where they had forgotten to take down our church notices from the bulletin boards!

Dear, timid Madame Fleischmann who had never even taught a Sunday school class, thought, "They have come to church. They must have something. I will ask the Holy Spirit to tell me what to do and say"—and stood up to explain to them *why* there was no pastor!

After giving this startling information she told them that she would help them to have a service, in spite of the fact that her English is far from perfect. "I prayed in English, and then in French—for I found a French family was present—then we sang together, and then I asked a nice-looking English lady to read from the book of John, as I thought the Word of God should be pronounced properly. Then I took your two sheets of Bible study on the resurrection and translated them into English, and French. Then we sang again and had prayer. I spoke of how it is necessary to take this risen Jesus as one's Saviour . . . and then I sang a little German benediction, as we had no pastor to give a benediction."

Debby, Susan and I were overwhelmed as we read this letter, and I said, "What thrilling stories there must be hidden in the heart of China and Russia, and many other places, which will one day be told in Heaven, where I am sure there will be endless time to trace the threads of His weaving!"

Les Dents du Midi

CHAPTER ELEVEN

The King's Heart
is in the Hand of the Lord

P RISCILLA ARRIVED home from her first week at the university to be greeted with shrieks of glee from Franky. "Did you come on the yellow bus? I have to go on the third bus."

He was always talking about the *third* bus those days, for some reason known only to himself.

That week a telephone call from Lausanne brought us the news that a *décision favorable* had been taken by the Committee on Religion and Education, so one more step had been given. Now the rest of the authorities would have to make their decision and then the whole dossier would go to Berne for the final word from the Federal Government. The news gave a temporary feeling of relief, but we knew there were many possibilities still of a negative conclusion. It was at least a mild case of living under a hanging axe.

We could not make any changes in the chalet, nor have a phone put in, until the permit were a more certain thing. The lack of a telephone meant that I had continually to be going next door with twenty or sixty centimes in my hand, to use the neighbours' phone. I discovered that these two maiden ladies had a little *pension*, and one of them also did embroidery which was photographed for a magazine. We exchanged a few sentences each time I went, and Debby frequently sought their help for difficulties she had in her school homework, as Priscilla was not there, and she was our only "authority" in French at that time.

One afternoon the two Mademoiselles asked me whether we would be staying long, and why we had come to Huémoz. I felt it was only fair to take the time to tell them the whole story.

As I was telling it they shook their heads, and looked at each other with shocked glances. "*Mais . . . mais . . .* we'll have to tell our brother about this."

"*Oui, oui . . .* we certainly will, I'll telephone him tonight."

"This surely can't be allowed, you shall surely *stay*."

I thanked them warmly and went home a bit puzzled, and not too impressed, thinking, "Dear ladies, wanting to do their best to help, and probably their brother is the one person who always 'fixes' things in their lives." It gave me a warm feeling that one gets when someone is being really thoughtful—but that was all.

When Alice the post-girl brought the mail the next morning, I asked her, "By the way, who is the brother of these two ladies who live in Beau Site?"

"Why don't you *know*?" she asked by way of response. "He's Monsieur Chaudet, the head of our national defence. He is one of the Council of Seven!"

I was duly impressed and drew in my breath with an exclamation of surprise. "*Really?* Well then he *could* do something."

"He certainly *could*, he is one of the alternating presidents of Switzerland."

The Swiss have no general election for their president, because their land is governed by an elected council of seven men. These seven men are each head of some department of the country, such as national defence, education and religion, health, and so forth. They are something like a Cabinet, and they become president in rotation. A man is president for a period of one year, and then the presidency rotates to another of the seven. It really is very democratic. At that time Monsieur Chaudet was President! The sisters calmly told me that they would telephone the President to tell him what had taken place!

Switzerland has twenty-two *cantons*, so from only seven of

them is there a man on this Council of Seven. Each *canton* has many cities and villages. The village of Huémoz had at that time seventy houses. In all the land, what a "coincidence" that we should have landed in a house next door to the sisters of one of the men on the Council of Seven!

Coincidence? Chance? Luck? It spoke to us of the One who could turn back the Red Sea, of the One who could shut lions' mouths.

A slightly bent little old man, with white hair and twinkly blue eyes, passed on the back road each day, as I was hanging up the wash. With a shovel and rake he went to his vegetable garden, a plot of land some distance from his chalet. We spoke to each other, and sometimes he stopped to talk a little longer. One day I thought it would be only fair to go to his home to tell him the story of what had brought us to that place, as Alice had told me he was a retired pastor, and a respected man in the village. He had not only been a pastor for many years, but this nature-loving, gentle man had also become a fully accredited Swiss mountain guide, having passed the difficult tests in his youth so as to be qualified to take young people on climbs without hiring an expensive guide.

It so happened that this pastor had trained a man from Champéry as his porter, and he had grown to love and trust this man. When we told our story to him, his reaction was to call his old porter, now a leading guide himself, and ask his opinion of the case. That Champéry guide turned out to be a fine friend, Mr. Avanthey, who gave a very favourable report concerning us and said in no uncertain terms that we had many friends in Champéry who were quite upset about our being put out!

The pastor turned to us in his deliberate way, a slow smile coming first to his lips and then his eyes, and said, "I will write to my nephew about this. I shall tell him the whole story, so that he may look into it."

And who was his nephew? He was the Chief of the department of the *Bureau des Etrangers* in Berne. He was the one who would do the final signing of anything to be signed concerning our permit. We found out later, through the pastor, that this man had been away when the edict against us had come through his office, and the assistant, who was Roman Catholic, had signed it. This man had power to sign papers when his superior officer was not there. But a thing of such importance and so contrary to normal procedure would not usually be signed without the Chief knowing about it.

This pastor was our neighbour . . . two doors away on the other side of Les Mélèzes! Who could choose such a chalet, situated between relatives of two such people? *Coincidence? Chance? Luck?* Again let me tell you we believed it to be a miracle of answered prayer, by a Personal God.

A few days later one of the Mademoiselles came over excitedly, saying as I opened the door, "Oh, we've had a letter from our brother, that just arrived now, and he says to tell you he looked into the matter yesterday, and it is now a settled question . . . you are to stay here! You may send a telegram to that effect to your American friends and family so that they will no longer be worried."

No higher word could have been given us, but we had to wait until June 21st before the actual permit was in our hands, and the passports were returned with "ANNULÉ, ANNULÉ, ANNULÉ" stamped in purple ink over the code numbers on a page which would otherwise have caused us to be put out of the country, and prevented from returning during that two-year period. ANNULLED! What a victory!

The difficulties of this period had been not only the un-certainty of the final outcome of the edict against us, and the uncertainty of that approaching moment when the total pay-ment on the chalet would need to be made, but a haunting feeling of being in a kind of "prison" as far as our work was concerned. Our passports were in the hands of the police (and remained there until June 21st); because of that fact, and of Franky and Susan, we had to let that Finnish trip stay cancelled. We really could not go back to Champéry during that time, so we could not go back to continue the evening discussion groups with the schools, nor to have the Sunday morning church. Here in Huémoz we had no apparent con-tact with boarding schools, and no children clamouring to come for Bible classes. What was our "work" going to be?

In spite of the thrilling answers which were piling up, there was this nagging, haunting question, "What are we here for? Why has God brought us to Chalet les Mélèzes, in the tiny village of Huémoz?"

As Priscilla listened on the phone to the exciting news about Mademoiselle Chaudet's assuring message from her brother in Berne, she could hardly wait to pour out her own news, and ask a question. "Oh, Mother, I've met an American girl, very voguish looking, sort of Grace Kelly looks, someone who stays aloof from the others. I never thought I'd meet her. Then the other day she just walked up to me after class and started talking about French. Suddenly she said, 'Your father's a pastor isn't he?' I don't know who could have told her that. 'I'm so mixed up myself I don't have any religion . . . and no one in my family has any stability. . . . I wish I could talk to your father.' We had a coffee together, and as we talked I realised that her questions, springing from Hinduism and Buddhism which she is studying with an oriental teacher here in Lausanne, need *Daddy's* answers. Oh, could I bring her home for the weekend? I know the chalet is still in a mess, but I don't think she'd mind!"

There was a thunderstorm going on that Friday when Grace and Priscilla arrived, and the electricity had gone off in the chalet. Two other girls had just arrived too, Dorothy Jamison, daughter of friends of ours in Los Angeles, and Ruth, a university friend with whom she was hitch-hiking.

That Friday night we sat around the dining-room table until the candles sputtered out. I fed Franky upstairs in his room, in between serving courses (a custom I started then and kept up for a couple of years, as discussions around the evening dinner table were apt to be hindered by a loquacious little boy, and he needed quiet and a bedtime story), and after dessert I disappeared to finish up Franky and to wash dishes. However, there was still plenty of time to get "in" on the discussion, as it went on until 2 a.m., right there around the table.

Saturday noon at lunch almost the same thing happened. A discussion commenced, questions poured forth, spontaneously and naturally—questions springing from oriental religions, from various philosophies, from the philosophies behind modern plays and art . . . and answers were carefully and thoughtfully given, showing the logical conclusion of various philosophies, and then going into the answers which the system taught in the Bible gives to the problems philosophers have struggled with through the ages.

Grace was astonished that we actually believed the Bible to be true. "Why, I thought that belief in the Bible went out with the Dark Ages. I didn't know anyone believed it to be true . . . not *today*."

The weekend went on with hikes and meals. Saturday night we built a fire outside on a bit of gravel terrace tucked under a rise of ground. There is a natural bank of grass in a semi-circle around this gravel, just perfect for crouching to toast hot dogs, and later to sit and talk around the fire. At that time there was a cobblestone open porch affair on ground level, where we spread a table buffet style. "In clear weather," we thought, "this will provide the place for talking, and solve the difficulty of at least one weekend meal to be cooked in those little stoves."

When Grace first went back to the university, she said she felt her world had been turned upside down, and she avoided Priscilla. Then she began seeking her out, and asking more questions, and talking to other students. Soon other students were talking to Priscilla about Christianity too, and another girl wanted to come up for a weekend, a girl from the southern part of the United States who had been seeking some sort of peace in making trips to shrines in Spain, although she had come from a Protestant background. The next girls to come were from Germany. And so it continued!

Meantime two young artists, girls who had won prizes in the form of travel to Europe, stopped to stay for a week, and in between sketching scenes in the village and mountains, they spent their time asking questions and listening to answers, either walking with Fran, or following me around the kitchen— or finding a discussion with Susan was a surprising experience.

As the end of May drew near, one thing was becoming

certain in our minds. God had brought us to this little village, at 3,100 feet altitude, to have a chalet which would be *L'Abri*, or The Shelter: not as a place to come to for evenings, as we had pictured at Champéry, but as a place to come to and stay, for a weekend or for a few days, as one would come to an open home as a guest; with time to ask questions and consider the answers during walks in the mountains, times around the meal tables, or informal moments in the kitchen. This had not been *our* plan, but as we prayed asking God to show us what He had brought us to Huémoz to do we became certain that He *was* showing us, day by day, and weekend by weekend.

Eight days before May 30th we had exactly $4,915.69 on the thermometer. The "thermometer" was a drawing of a thermometer on a piece of cardboard which Priscilla and Susan had made. Each gift that came in towards the payment on the chalet, they marked on this chart, and we all became more and more interested in seeing "what the Lord will do". That He *would* do it we felt sure, with a faith based on the certainty of those past signposts or markers. It seemed definite to us that God had been the One who had not only led us to the chalet, but who had led us to promise to buy it, and had amazingly placed us where the needed help had been given towards our having the permit to stay. Surely He would not fail us in this imperative moment when just the right amount of money was needed? *If* we were correct in believing that He had a special purpose in bringing us to this chalet, then this "impossible" request we were making in prayer, for the exact amount of money, $7,366, to be in our hands for the payment, would also be answered. It became a bit tense at moments, but really there were no great deluges of doubt at that time. He had already shown us that this whole matter was not in our hands, we felt. Each mail brought a new jump to the thermometer those last days, and new causes for rejoicing. Some were very little "jumps" and humanly it looked increasingly impossible, but at that particular time we had an amazing inner peace, before the answer was seen. "The peace of God", which the Bible says "passes all understanding", is a marvellous thing to experience. It really is His peace and not ours, a supernatural thing. After all "super" just means "above" . . . and it is something just "above" or out of the usual.

Saturday, Susan's birthday, was celebrated with a hot dog roast to which two wide-eyed village children came, never having seen such a procedure before. And Sunday, just as we finished eating dinner, the yellow bus stopped, emptying out three ladies who made their way up the steps. One was Madame Fleischmann, who had brought a bag with her precious securities in it, truly "the widow's mite" . . . "in case you need to borrow it tomorrow". The two others were from Lakeland, Florida, and had just come to Geneva by plane with 350 other women for a Women's Club convention and tour of Europe. There were enough leftovers to warm up and make a second dinner. While I talked to the ladies as they were eating, Franky slept, Priscilla talked to one of the artists, Susan talked to Madame Fleischmann, and Fran brought the conversations of the week to a conclusion with Phyllis, the other artist who was leaving on the next bus.

"I'm not sure what Christianity meant to me before, but I know now what it means to me," she said earnestly as she accepted Christ as her Saviour and prayed. Her face was radiant, as she boarded the bus, but no more radiant than the feeling we had as we thrilled over this "new birth" in Chalet Mélèzes, just twenty-four hours before payment time! Could we doubt that God had shown us that He was going to use *L'Abri* for His own purposes, and that He would make the purchase of the necessary house possible?

WEDNESDAY AUGUST 14, 1968
L'ABRI DAY of PRAYER

JESUS ANSWERED AND SAID UNTO THEM, VERILY I SAY
UNTO YOU, IF YE HAVE FAITH AND DOUBT NOT, YE SHALL
NOT ONLY DO THIS WHICH IS DONE UNTO THE FIG TREE,
BUT ALSO IF YE SHALL SAY UNTO THIS MOUNTAIN, BE
THOU REMOVED AND

	PRAYER ROOM		OTHER PLACES
SIGN		8:30–9:00	J.S.S
UP	Jackie	9:00–9:30	
FOR	ayn	9:30–10:00	Nancy
YOUR		10:00–10:30	
TIME	J PS	10:30–11:00	Frankie S
OF	Christina	11:00–11:30	P Davies
PRAYER	Baby R	11:30–12:00	Abby
	NB	12:00–12:30	OG
	B.C.	12:30–1:00	Hilda Perkinmachen
	Michael W.	1:00–1:30	John S.
	E.S.S.	1:30–2:00	
	Connie	2:00–2:30	Ray Weaver
	Cynthia	2:30–3:00	Fred
	Wilda	3:00–3:30	FAS
	J.D.Wysor	3:30–4:00	Os
	Sylvia	4:00–4:30	
	Larry	4:30–5:00	D.S.M.
	Barbara	5:00–5:30	
	VWM	5:30–6:00	
	Cora	6:00–6:30	Jane S Smith
		6:30–7:00	

BE THOU CAST INTO THE SEA;
IT SHALL BE DONE. AND ALL THINGS, WHATSOEVER
YE SHALL ASK IN PRAYER, BELIEVING, YE SHALL RECEIVE.
MATT. 21:21,22

CHAPTER TWELVE

The Step of Faith answered

T HERE WAS a cheering sun the morning of May 30th, 1955, as Franky and I ran down to the village for fresh bread for breakfast, and I felt an inner surge of excitement as time for the "last mail" approached. The "'merican girls" as Franky called the ladies from Florida (to their delight), were having a late breakfast on the balcony, when Alice came with the mail. "Look, look, look," cried Alice, cheeks flushed and blue eyes dancing with pleasure. "Lots of letters. See?" She was excited because she knew of our praying for the money for the payment, and she knew Fran and Priscilla would be taking the two o'clock bus for Aigle, to make the payment. It was then eleven in the morning!

Hurrying back to the breakfast table on the balcony, we shared the exciting contents of those fifteen letters with Madame Fleischmann and the Florida ladies, as cheques tumbled out, and the reading of letters brought tales of how people had been led to send various amounts. The fifteen gifts of that morning amounted to $814 to be added to the total.

We all went down to the ground floor bedroom which was now being used for a make-shift living-room, and had a thanksgiving prayer meeting. It hadn't been possible . . . but it had happened! Two months before Priscilla had printed on the thermometer "And His name shall be called WONDERFUL, COUNSELLOR . . ." (Isaiah 9:6) which Handel set to music in

The Messiah. We could have sung it that morning with tremendous feeling! It was a moment of deep emotion.

Incidentally, Madame Fleischmann did *not* need to lend a penny of her securities to us, nor did anyone have to make up the last of the amount.

It was evening before I heard the rest of the story of that day. At Aigle, when the ladies changed trains, and Fran and Priscilla turned to go to the notary's office, Mrs. K. said to Fran, "I have done what you told me to," with a sincerity and spontaneity that was very real. It sounds almost like a "touched up" story, but it isn't. It is just a demonstration of how God sometimes underlines events when we have prayed with honesty for His guidance.

This seemed to be saying to us, as from Him, "I chose this chalet, I have guided in the purchase of it, I have sent in the needed amount of money for today's transaction, and *this* is the way I am going to use it, to help people who have spiritual need."

The first thing handed to them as they arrived at the notary's office was a special delivery letter. It contained a letter of encouragement, and thanks for all that he had received spiritually, from Mr. Ex., along with a gift—"enclosed is something that will give me a small share in the purchase of the house today." As all expenses were added up, including taxes and the notary's fee, the total was within three dollars of being exact.

The fact that there was not too much was just as amazing as the fact that there was enough. Think of it for a moment. Over a two-month period of time, about 157 gifts came from very scattered places on the earth's surface. No one could consult with anyone else as to what his or her gift would do in the total. The smallest gift was $1, and except for that first gift of a thousand dollars, the largest was $225. The total came to exactly $7,343.30. We had figured that we needed $7,366, including all fees, but there were a few of the settlement fees that we found would be a bit smaller than we expected, so when all the mathematics was finished it was within three dollars of being exact! The bank gave the mortgage, and the amount to be paid monthly towards the mortgage payments would be less than any rent we could have had in that section of the mountains. Amazingly enough, not one gift came late! From that time on not another gift came to us designated for the buying of the house.

The whole experience of those weeks, and this final result, was to be to us a demonstration of what God could do in answer to prayer. But it was not simply to end in a full stop. It was not to be something we would look *back* to and say, "We know, because way back there we had specific answers to prayer . . . way back when . . ."

Young people were coming weekends. It never stopped, but increased week by week. These young people were seeking answers to life: "Is there any purpose to life?" "Is there meaning in the universe?" "Where does personality come from?" They were coming from many different backgrounds, but almost without exception they were unbelievers when they came. Most of them either felt there was not any God, or were not sure whether God existed or not. Answers were given to their questions. Careful, long, thorough answers from an intellectual base. Then positive teaching was also given, teaching based on the Bible.

But in addition to these conversations and discussions, something else was happening. People were finding it hard to "shake off" what they were living through. They were *there* while we were praying for things that they later found had been given. Just as Alice the post-girl had become involved in the intense waiting for the answer concerning the permit, and the buying of the house, so had others. They were being given (*not by us* but by God's answers to prayers) a demonstration that God exists . . . a demonstration of the fact that He is there. It was a combination that *we* had not planned, or dreamed up, but which God had given. It was a combination which could never be "planned" or "put on" as an exhibit . . . it had to be real.

Now we felt that God was using this not only to help the young people who were coming and going at that time, but also to say something to us about the future. He had given us a series of signposts or markers on the trail . . . but those markers did not lead us simply to stay in Switzerland in a new location, they led us to a completely new work. We realise now that the work which *L'Abri* became would never have been possible if we had not been uprooted completely in every way, and if in that uprooting we had not decided to pray for God's solution and leading every step of the path as it wound through unknown territory.

As June 4th came, only five days after the payment had been made, we reached a decision. Rather than having the buying of the chalet become a "full stop" to the last paragraph of a chapter, we felt it *must* be the opening of a new chapter altogether. So we sat down and resigned from the mission board under which we had served, and from which we received a monthly salary. We stated that we believed that the Lord was leading us to establish *L'Abri Fellowship*.

Had we gone crazy? With responsibilities just taken on for mortgage payments, with one daughter in university and three children at home, what did we expect to live on? and to feed ourselves with?

This is what we felt we were being led to do: to ask God that our work, and our lives, be a demonstration that He does exist; not just for six weeks, not for three months, but for as long as He would continue to lead us to live in this manner. We set forth the following principles upon which we expected to establish *L'Abri Fellowship*:

1. We said we would pray that God would send the people of His choice to us, and keep away any who would only be coming to ski or to "take advantage" of an open home. We felt only God could choose the right ones to come, as only God can see the hearts. This to us was as much asking for a miracle, as the asking for material things.

2. We said we would pray that God would send, week by week, and month by month, enough money to care for our needs as a family, *and* for food and so on for those whom He would send us to help. We felt that both the spiritual food, and the physical food, should be freely given, as to any guests in a home.

Let me explain. When members of your family invite someone home for a weekend, do you present a bill at the end of the weekend? Of course not. Each one who came to *L'Abri* came as a guest of Priscilla's, or of one of those who had already come several times, and who felt "at home" too. The whole informality of an "open home" would have been destroyed the moment we put a "price" on it, and turned it into a kind of hotel, youth hostel, or a religious conference centre of some sort. We felt that the relaxed feeling people had, and the openness with which they were ready to ask questions, was partly due to the fact that there was no air of an institution about the place, and we wanted to keep it that way if at all possible, for as long as possible.

3. We said we would not have a plan, but pray for the direct leading of God, in various ways, to give us His plan for the work. We were willing to have it always be just a handful of people avidly asking questions and seriously thinking, but if it were to grow or change in any way, we said we wanted a demonstration of the fact that God is able in the twentieth century to give a plan that is fresh and unique, that it is not necessary to follow along in the ruts of "the way it has always been done". Among other things we were sure that in this way the work would be prepared for the needs of the future, and not just be meeting the needs of the past.

4. We also prayed that if it grew, God would send us the Workers of His choice, rather than our trying to advertise or get people to help us.

Usually Christian work is mapped out by committees and boards, gathered together for that purpose. Usually groups are gathered together by some kind of intensive advertising, by printed folders, radio announcements, and so on. Usually there is a drive to get as many people as possible gathered together wherever they are being gathered, and numbers mean a lot.

So *not* to advertise, but simply to pray that God will send those of His choice, and keep others away, is a *different* way of doing things. We don't say everyone ought to work this way, we simply say we feel we were led by God to do this as a demonstration that He is able to bring the people to a place— even a tiny out-of-the-way place like an unheard-of mountain village—and only to bring the ones He wants to have there for His purposes.

Usually money is raised for Christian causes by collections taken in churches and missionary meetings to meet the needs or obligations. People are urged to give, and the needs are told them. Sometimes pressure is put on. You probably know how money is asked for, and sometimes even begged for. The charitable organisations have various ways of getting pledges of money, as well as the religious organisations. We are not saying these people are wrong, nor are we criticising them. We are simply saying that simply to pray for money is different from the usual way funds are raised.

What happens when you pray? God is all powerful in every realm. He can do things in a variety of ways, but one way in which He works is to "move" in the realm of men's minds. God can place an idea in a person's mind. He can cause someone to feel a strong "urge" or "conviction" to do something. So when we pray for a certain amount of money, God can cause one person to reach for a cheque-book and send that amount, or He can cause a dozen people to send odd fractions of that amount, causing the total to be exact. You may not believe that He does this, but I am simply saying that when I talk about praying for money, *this* is what I mean.

Yes, usually the result is that other human beings give "donations", but they have not been asked to, and they have not received an envelope to fill, and they have not had human pressure put on them to give. They give because they feel God has led them to give, and often their having been led gives them an exciting feeling of having been in communication with God, in the *same* way as it does when the "answer" comes to prayer, and you know God has heard and acted in space, and time, and history. You know then that your communication has not been an airy-fairy sort of psychological communication into the atmosphere, but that you have contacted a *Person*, who has replied.

It is a good thing to have an orderly "plan" for a work, in many cases. People plan out work for years in advance. They plan a school, a way of reaching into a whole country, town by town, with everything from insurance sales to religion. It's the way it is usually done. You might say that in human circles everywhere it is the "done thing" to have a human plan ahead of time: a clever one, an intelligent one.

Now again, let me say, we don't think there is anything wrong with people working according to plan. It's just that in our desire to be used in our work, our lives should be a demonstration of the fact that God exists and this was involved too. In fact it is one of the basic "involvements". If God exists, He is the One with infinite intelligence, infinite wisdom, infinite knowledge, infinite judgement. He would know how to plan a work, how to use lives, beyond any human being. We felt then that it would be possible to place our individual lives, and our "work" of the future, into His planning. We felt it would be possible for Him to communicate day by day, week by week, month by month, this plan of His to us.

Did we expect to have a blueprint? No. As you have seen in the story of those few weeks, we had no idea at times what was coming in the next few hours, let alone a week ahead. That was an intense time, more intense than usual, but we've had a lot of sudden surprises in God's planning of *L'Abri*. We've seen developments that we had never visualised. I can't emphasise too strongly that we really did not have a clue as to what was ahead, except that we felt God was beginning to send to us people who needed help.

Here we were then in the beginning of June 1955, a family of six people. One man, one woman, one girl of nearly eighteen, one girl of just fourteen, one girl who'd had her tenth birthday, and a little boy who would not be three until August, living in a chalet by the side of the road in a tiny village, that cars speed through on their way to the ski resort above.

They have just cut themselves off from any organisational help. Their work is to pray that God will send them the people of His choice, and to receive these people, caring for them as they come, as guests. They are going to pray for their financial needs to be met. They have thrown out tin cans and bottles by the hundred from the long uncared for property, and have planted a garden which may give them some food by August. But otherwise they have no source of supply.

What is going to happen?

CHAPTER THIRTEEN

A Plan unfolds

THAT VERY week the C.'s arrived to stay some days to rest. The strain of the death of their baby had been increased by a tremendous disappointment in the fact that the permission given in Czechoslovakia for his mother to come and visit her grandchild, had been revoked, because there was no grandchild. We felt they needed special shelter at that time.

What a week it turned out to be! On Friday at lunchtime the dining-room table was full (at that period we thought a full table and a full dining-room consisted of about ten or eleven people—later that came to be what we called "a small family"). As I was about to empty a bowl of beaten eggs and milk into a frying pan to make an omelet, while the people ate their soup, a knock came at the front door, and there were two girls from Virginia.

"Come on out into the kitchen with me," I invited, "and we can talk while I make an omelet. What did you say your names were? Anne and Mary?" From that day to this, I never speak of one of those girls without speaking of them both, Anne and Mary they were, and are!

Anne and Mary had come to Basle, Switzerland, to commence a school of occupational therapy for the big hospital there. They were both Christians, and their desire was not simply to teach occupational therapy, but to engage in serious conversation with their students, nurses, anyone with whom they happened to come into contact, because they believed, as we do, that God's truth matters, and they also believed the Bible to be true. We exchanged "histories" of what we had been doing, and were doing. They exclaimed, "May we come back in August, and bring a nurse who is interested, but who is not a Christian?"

That commenced a whole "skein" of threads that are to be woven in and out of the story of our work, and of a variety of projects elsewhere being carried on by people whose lives have been changed. Anne and Mary came back, the nurse came with them, and she became a Christian. They brought students studying with them, Danish girls, English girls, Swiss girls, German girls, American girls, Jewish girls, atheistic girls. They brought a carful each time they came, and because of the limited space, we had to spread mattresses on the living-room floor all that first year, and then quickly take up the bedding on Sunday morning, and rearrange the room for "church".

They felt they had had an answer to prayer in the fact that we were there, and that such a thing as *L'Abri* had come into existence just when they needed it for what they were hoping to do. We felt their coming, and the contacts with medical people through them, was an answer to prayer as we asked God to bring those of His choice to us. We marvelled at how evident it was that *we* had not planned this but that it *had* been planned.

Just let me follow the central thread of this complex of threads to show you what I mean. After three years, Anne and Mary, and Rosemary (an occupational therapist who had become a Christian at *L'Abri*) felt that they should turn over the leadership of the school to Swiss, as there were Swiss people ready to carry on. Rosemary went back to California to fill a position, Anne and Mary came to be *L'Abri* Workers, temporarily, as they wanted time to pray for God's guidance as to what they should do next. Both of them had interesting and lucrative positions offered them in other countries, but they wanted to be sure as to God's will.

During the girls' time with us the big chalet next door—

which you may remember I told you was empty when I first saw Les Mélèzes—was put up for sale. It had not stayed empty, as a Roman Catholic organisation had bought it and was using it for a children's rest home. Often our hot dog roasts and discussions had an accompaniment of the chanting of masses being said next door. It presented a problem, which we had been praying about. Then the house was put up for sale. . . .

It was a huge place. It had been a small hotel to start with. Anne and Mary looked at it. They told us that it was amazing to them, because they had been praying about a specific thing, which they felt to be a need in Switzerland. They had been praying about starting a home for cerebral palsy children. They felt that a new therapy they knew of would be a great help to the children physically, and they also had a deep desire to help these handicapped children spiritually. "We wondered whether it would be possible to have such a place near you, so that not only the children, but nurses and other helpers we would need to have, could benefit from the spiritual help of *L'Abri*. And now to have a chalet for sale next door seems to be a kind of sign?"

They had no money, but they believed very definitely that if God wanted them to undertake this project, and if He meant them to do it in this Chalet Bellevue next door to us, then He would make it possible. They didn't just sit back and wait, though. They prayed earnestly, and made all sorts of inquiries as to the necessary medical requirements and laws involved in opening such a home. I can't possibly tell you their whole story, or it would be a book within a book . . .!

Just peer back with me into one spring afternoon, as a tiny sample. Anne and Mary had prayed for a certain amount of money by a certain date, necessary for their first payment. In addition they had prayed that someone would come to be a *L'Abri* Worker in their place, *before* they took any definite step in leaving us.

That spring afternoon the amount of money came, and in the mail which good old Alice brought was a letter written in the ticket booth of a theatre in England. It was from a ballet dancer who had become a Christian at the chalet a year before, and who now was pleading, "May I please come to the chalet as a Worker? I'll do anything, scrub floors . . . anything, but I have come to the conclusion that this is not the place for growing and deepening in my spiritual life. I don't think I'm really going to be able to reach others, as I hoped to, by continuing in this."

Anne and Mary were standing on the gravel outside, talking about the fact that the money had come. Alice the post-girl had just stopped to speak a few minutes with them too, when I ran out waving the letter with Linette's bold scrawl, "Look . . . look . . . look . . . here's your answer, Linette wants to come. She's the person God has moved to take your place, even though she doesn't know a thing about your praying for someone!"

Yes, their story would make another book: the preparation of that big place, the hard, hard work, the sacrificial lives they've led in caring for their patients, not during "hospital hours" but during "mothers' hours" . . . a twenty-four-hour-day sort of care. Rosemary turned down a tremendous offer in San Francisco to come and help them get started. The three of them are there still, along with nurses, other therapists and helpers. They have seventeen cerebral palsy children ranging in age from six months to twenty years of age, from Switzerland and also from other countries, and ranging in degree of handicap. Children have been physically helped, and spiritually helped, and have become a blended-together "family". The place has changed and has become better equipped as the years have gone by, but the hard, hard work continues. It is not a money-making proposition.

Why do the girls do it? Because they really believe that God has led them into this as His plan for them, as well as part of their warm concern and love for this needy group of children.

But standing there and serving the omelet and salad as Anne and Mary helped me relay food to the dining-room that day, only a few days after we had made our decision to ask God to make our work a demonstration of His existence, we didn't know any of this, it was all hidden "future" to us then. When

Anne and Mary hurried out to their car, afraid they'd be late for their appointment, we said simply, "We'll see you again in August!" and turned back to a job of dishwashing!

Priscilla burst in a couple of hours later with four coming from the university for the weekend—Liza, Grace, Margaret and Evelyn. Conversation around the dinner table lasted till after midnight, and as for sleeping arrangements . . . an American couple had the double decker bunk room, the university girls had the four-bed bedroom, someone else was in the little end room which has a narrow single bed, a big window, a door out to the breakfast end of the balcony, and glass doors into the hall, and practically no floor space—but a magnificent view! So we had to rent a room in the *pension* next door for the C.'s to rest in. That was how the first week got started!

Later in June the yellow bus brought two fellows who apparently had come together. However, we found that they had only met in Aigle, where Karl, coming from an American Army base in Germany, was trying to buy a ticket to Huémoz, and as he had no Swiss francs and did not know French, was having a bit of difficulty. John stepped up and offered to pay for the ticket, and they walked off towards the little train together, making a discovery—they were both headed for the same place!

Karl, a Christian fellow from our church in St. Louis, was coming to visit us for the first time in Europe. John, a Swiss fellow brought up in Scarsdale, New York, and with an American citizenship, had been casually asked by Grace, "Why don't you come up to Huémoz with me this weekend? There's a nice American family there, sort of a house party. You'd like it." And then as she met him at the train it was only to say breathlessly, "You go on" (as the train started), "I'm coming up later with Dick on his motor-bike." So that was all the information John had.

Fran met them at the gate, thinking they both knew about *L'Abri*, and said, "Let's go for a walk, and talk."

As they started off something was said about Christianity and John came out with this innocent question: "Oh, I don't think Christianity has a leg to stand on, intellectually, do you, Mr. Schaeffer?"

He had a two-hour answer given him, which must have startled him. That was the first question he asked his future father-in-law!

John's dark lashed blue eyes became filled with thoughtfulness and interest as the weekend went on, and he listened intently to the answers being given to an atheist at the hot dog roast that night. I remember looking down on that group seated on worn quilts around the campfire, with an old oil lantern giving just enough light to read verses from the open Bible, when they were needed. I stood where I could hear Franky call, as I wasn't sure he was asleep yet, and prayed for the ones gathered down below, that God, who could look penetratingly into the minds and hearts, would give "light" for the "eyes of understanding".

These were the "eyes" John was talking about when he wrote in the guest book the next evening, "My eyes have been opened to a new world in which I hope to dwell with a coming faith!"

John's a thorough sort of person. He took the twenty-five basic Bible studies and made a careful study that summer, and we didn't see him until the fall. It was November when he came up with others from the university and during a walk on the Panex road, with the pine trees towering above them, he said to Fran, "I've put my foot down." Meaning that he had made a definite decision, and had in a very real sense put his "foot" in the circle of "life", having taken it out of the circle of "death". For the Bible says that to believe in the Lord Jesus is to have life eternal, which is the opposite of death.

To bring you swiftly up to date on John. He and Priscilla both graduated from the University of Lausanne, then John studied in St. Louis, taking two theological degrees (in four years) while Priscilla, who was his wife by then, taught French in a girls' school. Now both of them, along with their tiny daughters Elizabeth and Rebecca, are in a chalet on the back road, helping in the *L'Abri* work of the present, with their chalet as full, most of the time, as ours.

A continuity can be seen in God's plan as it unfolded, a continuity which would have been beyond our planning, if we had tried to map out such a work ourselves. It seems to me that the way things developed as a whole, as well as the individual answers to prayer, also point to the actions of a Person who exists, and who is able to carry out the promises He makes to His children in His Word.

Karl Woodson kept coming back, bringing others from the Army during his time in Europe. Then he came to be a *L'Abri* Worker for a summer. It was that summer that Alida Meester, daughter of a Dutch pastor, was a Worker. Tying up pea vines, weeding the lettuces, taking the milk pails to the village together, Karl and Alida were one of *L'Abri*'s romances, which culminated in a wedding in Holland the following spring. They are now *L'Abri* representatives in America, and Karl is Assistant Treasurer of *L'Abri*. John became the Treasurer.

At the end of that first June, we had been in the chalet only three months, and we still had not had the electricity voltage changed. The hum of the refrigerator and washing machine were not heard until September, when suddenly also the electric sockets became things of usefulness, as plugging in an iron at *last* brought heat.

Our first Worker was Dorothy Jamison. She was at *L'Abri* the first weekend Priscilla brought Grace. She had her college degree, and was working towards her Master's in Psychology, but she felt she wanted to come back and "listen in" on more of those discussions, and also be a part of the "living by prayer" that we had set out to do. She thought she might stay for a few months, but in the end she stayed for two years!

The second year she was with us, was the year that Hurvey Woodson (Karl's brother) came over to spend a year as a *L'Abri* Worker, interrupting his theological studies with a time he felt would be more profitable, a time of listening in on live discussions with people of so many backgrounds and philosophies, as well as talking to people himself, and helping with the practical side of the work.

That year ended up in a very happy wedding in the living-room, decked with 500 big daisies to look like a garden. It might have ended up in a terrible mistake, with two people going far from each other, never to meet again, who were both in love but who each thought the other didn't like them! Happily the misunderstanding was discovered, and the lovely quiet wedding took place, and they went back to America, together.

It was July that Dorothy came, and it was July that we became officially *L'Abri Fellowship*, with someone representing us in America. My father, Dr. George H. Seville, a former missionary to China with the China Inland Mission, was just retiring from his position as a professor in a theological school. He wrote to us offering to do the work of a "Home Secretary", without accepting any remuneration for it. He said he felt he would like that to be his gift to the work of *L'Abri*. Although he was in his eightieth year, he took on the work of caring for any legal matters, of receiving and transmitting gifts. My mother addressed envelopes, and arranged for the letters to be duplicated giving the month by month story of the work. They began "Dear Family", with my own family in mind, but then continued as the "family" grew.

The fact that they were in a position to do all this, and had the knowledge of what needed to be done, seemed another specific answer to a need before the need had even been thought about. It meant that there was no necessity to go to America to care for any of these details.

It wouldn't be honest just to hit high points of prayer answers and assurances, without giving some of the reality of the accompanying struggles and difficulties. Anyone who pictures a life based on the determination to live hour by hour in the reality of the existence of God as a life that is carefree, happy, and without problems, has not really experienced reality, I feel. The Bible teaches that there is a conflict in the universe. One day, in the future, that conflict will end in victory. That day has not yet come. Our present experience in looking around the world, and the universe, is of finding evidence of two Personalities at conflict . . . God, and Satan. Satan is anxious to hold all the human beings he can under his power, in any one of a multitude of ways. Anyone who is openly intending to live on the basis of the existence of God, will find himself challenged, in a variety of ways. The challenges can be big or nagging, small things. The bigger crises are often the easiest to live through, while the smaller, nagging things are like mosquitoes nipping away, until you are tempted to run.

People came one after another. Wonderful! But it meant that family life was almost non-existent, except as an "enlarged" family.

Franky was having his third birthday, enjoying the fulfilment of his requests: "I want a blue cake, a horn and a swale." Not being able to find a whale, which we supposed he meant, we gave him a red fish to float in his bath, and he asked a bit curiously, "Is this a swale?"

At the beginning of the celebration one guest came on the early afternoon yellow bus, and so another chair was drawn up to the birthday table. Before the celebration was finished, the late afternoon bus arrived, and Pookie, a Buddhist from Siam (studying in Switzerland), ran up the steps. A glamorous oriental beauty, Pookie, from a prominent family, had been sent to a convent school. Now Roman Catholic teaching and Buddhist were mixed up in her thinking, and she almost wept as she said, "I really want to know *truth*, and my sister has become an atheist in a university in the States, but I'm not satisfied with her reasoning either. I wouldn't have come if I hadn't really wanted to ask questions!"

The next evening Pookie, the other guest, and Fran were walking and talking, Priscilla and Dot were doing dishes, and I had decided to do a rare thing: go to bed early and read! Then the phone rang and four American college boys announced that they had at last reached the village, having hiked up a "short cut" through the woods from Ollon in the dark, because one of them had mistaken "fifty minutes" to be "five minutes", by muddling up his French! So when the "walking conversation" returned, they found an increased "family" gathered around the dining-room table munching cookies—and it turned into a long evening after all!!

We soon discovered that *L'Abri* wasn't going to be easy. But we hadn't asked for ease. We had asked for *reality*.

CHAPTER FOURTEEN

The First Year becomes History

THAT FIRST summer we prayed for a place, in addition to the dining-room and the outdoors (which would soon be too chilly), where we might have a homelike atmosphere for the long discussions. The real need was for a living-room with a fireplace. The answer came before we expected it.

Deep in the southern part of the United States a tuberculosis specialist read some of the "Family Letters" telling of *L'Abri*. These had been handed him by his cousin, who knew of his interest in Christian things. He himself was struggling for a greater reality in his life. Two things happened to him shortly after that. He felt definitely that God would have him send a certain amount to *L'Abri*, which in turn corresponded with what we needed to make a living-room. And secondly he himself, and his family, commenced a very sacrificial and unusual medical work in the southern mountains.

Some days later, another exciting gift arrived. It was designated for a fireplace, and came from Dr. Koop, head of a children's hospital, in an eastern state of the United States. He said he had been following the story of *L'Abri*, and felt as though his own faith had been tested as he held back from giving a gift for the buying of the house, "feeling the need to trust God to be *able* to do it, without me". Now he wrote that he wanted to give so that a fireplace might be built.

With those two amounts of money in hand, we sent for

Mr. Dubi, the carpenter, who began working with us as we planned a room, with the wall cut down, throwing those two ground floor bedrooms into one room. The fact that the chimney fitted in with the original structure of the house so that we could put a fireplace at one end of the room, and that the dividing wall held no weight, surprised Mr. Dubi. Details were so exciting in those days.

There was a sagging ceiling to correct with beaverboard and then cross-beams, there was a worn floor to re-cover with new wood. There were bookcases to build in, and old sagging furniture to make over and cover. Our dish barrel, stained dark brown, and made into a chair with red leather, became the chair Fran was to sit in to talk, hours on end. Plaid wool drapes were made, and cushions covered, out of the drapes we had made for Chalet Bijou's living-room. Gradually a room with personality grew into being.

But through it all people kept coming. Students from Lausanne who came weekend after weekend felt they had lived through the growth of that room, through all the praying for it, and the work of it, and they left at the end of their year of study feeling as though they were leaving home.

Were there only students from Lausanne, that first year, and the medical people from Basle? Let me try to give you some idea of the variety of people, without giving boring lists. There was a day in late August when a Mrs. J. arrived with her son J., twelve years old, having come with a desire that the boy find a strong reality and belief that would fortify him for difficulties she foresaw in the future for him. She had invited an Austrian university student who had been an exchange student in her town in America. Gunther soon had a room-mate however.

On September 9th, I was picking Thomas Laxton peas in the pouring rain, when a very American "hi" caused me to look up, startled, with water running down my face.

"I'm Bill, and I didn't wait for the bus . . . just hitch-hiked up from Ollon."

Bill, born the same year as Gunther, but half the world away on the west coast of America, had written a few weeks earlier from an American Army post in Germany, where he was serving his two years. "I hear you have a place where people come, and I'd like to come for a few days."

So blond, tall, blue-eyed Bill listened in to Gunther's questions being answered, listened further as the girls from Basle drove in with a carful of people, and was also there when the *L'Abri* library was amazingly increased with 200 books.

As the rain continued the next day, a Swiss man from Ollon stopped to ask if we would go with him to see his grandfather and grandmother's chalet on the back road. He was hoping we would buy it to meet our need for more space (that was one of the times that God's answer was "no", as no money came for the purchase of a second place). In addition to wanting to show us the chalet, he wanted to present us with his grandfather's Christian books: 200 fine old volumes which showed us that years before this Swiss–English family had lived on our back road, believing strongly the same truth, and buying, reading and loaning books to people which would deepen their knowledge of the Bible. Bill helped us to carry boxes of these books through the rain dripping from the trees that had seen the same books go *up* the road, carried by another generation, who little dreamed that they were preparing a library for *L'Abri*.

Fog and rain never did clear away sufficiently to give Bill a view of the mountains before he left, but he had seen more important things, and left saying, "Boy, I'm sure glad to have found a place where all a fellow's questions can be answered . . . and I'm sure going to bring a lot of others here."

Which remark, carried out, brought a stream of G.I.s during their "three day passes", in Bill's old car, and some G.I.s went home from Germany as Christians.

By November the little nucleus of interested students in the University of Lausanne asked Fran if he could come down once a week to have a discussion group there. That was the beginning of a most unusual discussion group and Bible class.

A little back room was found in a café—windowless, because the café is built against the same hill upon which the university buildings and cathedral stand. Permeated by the noise of a juke box, the room was not ideal in any aesthetic sense, but it had an atmosphere conducive to student discussion. There was nothing ecclesiastical about it to frighten anyone away at first glance. People came bringing their own sandwiches, to buy coffee or other beverages, and sat deep in thought, or aggressive in debate, for three hours, from eleven to two o'clock—the lunch period at that time. (Schedules changed in later years to shorten it to two hours.) There were the first ones who had come to *L'Abri*, and others with whom they had been talking. The first month found people from the United States, Holland, Germany, England, Canada, Greece, Portugal. And as time went on as many as twelve countries would be represented at once. There were people of many different religious, or non-religious, backgrounds. There were existentialists, humanists, liberal Jews, Roman Catholics, liberal Protestants, agnostics, and many other shades of thought represented. Some were very belligerent.

"So you believe all those myths really took place? You just start with the Bible, and go on from there?" someone would ask.

And the reply from Fran would be something like this at times, "Wait a minute, you have to start farther back . . . it is first of all a question of the meaning of personality in the universe. Let us imagine that the universe is entirely solids and water, no air in all the universe. All right then, you have fish living in this water for centuries. Then one of these fish by chance develops lungs that need air. Is this progress? Is this an improvement? No, the fish would drown because it would no longer be fitted to its environment.

"You think you have an explanation of the universe that suits you. Have you an adequate explanation that tells you the origin of that which you know best, *yourself*? Where did personality come from in the universe? Where did appreciation of beauty, the possibility of saying 'it is right', 'it is wrong', come from? Where did morality come from? What is it beyond biological attraction that makes it meaningful for a man to say 'I love you' to a woman?

"Let's not ask first of all 'is the Bible true?' Let's first see what the basic questions are, and find what the system taught in the Bible has in the way of answers."

That might be a beginning of the three hours!

Late in November another amazing bit of the Lord's plan was unfolded to us as a letter was brought by Alice in the afternoon mail. I took it into the dining-room where Madame Marclay and I were sewing, making drapes for the slowly developing living-room.

"Look, Madame Marclay, a letter from England from the travel agency asking whether or not we are going to have the usual holiday services in Champéry. They say they will be conducting a large group to Champéry during the holidays and would appreciate services in English."

"Oh, Madame Schaeffer you *must* come. I'm going to ask my husband about it."

We ourselves would never have thought of asking permission to go back for services so soon. But this was unsought-for, a request from a completely innocent source—a travel agency which did not know we had been put out of the village. We "spread that letter before the Lord".

The retired pastor "just happened" to drop in for a friendly call a day or two after that. "A little bird told me that you were working too hard, Madame Schaeffer, I've come to scold you a bit."

Then, "What do you hear from Champéry these days—anything new?"

I told him of the request from England, and he said, with more certainty than Madame Marclay, "Ah, you must go, you have every right to go, it is in the interest of liberty that you must be allowed to go. I feel so strongly about this that I shall write a letter to Sion reminding them of the liberty Roman Catholics enjoy in our Protestant *canton*. They know me in Sion." He nodded his head, eager to get back home to begin composing the letter.

We did nothing about the matter but pray. However, much was said about it by various people, and in the end it was brought to the Council of Seven of the village of Champéry. Mr. Ex. left the room, as he felt they could discuss it freely without him, so six of the seven came to the vote. And it was almost unanimous, in spite of the dissenting arguments, that we were to come back for services during that holiday season.

Such a dancing around and pinching each other that took place in our family as the news came. "Why, the chapel won't be dark a *single* season. The services are going to continue without a break since 1949. It's impossible, but it's happened."

The only cloud over the children's excitement was the fact that Susan could not come with us—she was in bed again with another attack of rheumatic fever.

The trip to Champéry was made in the Volkswagen or station-wagon taxi, and we sang carols lustily all the way over, stopping to pray with thanksgiving at the Rhône river, before crossing into Valais. We arrived to find the church full of smoke and the janitress rushing around opening windows to let out smoke and let in icy air, kicking the draught open and shut by turns and stuffing briquets in the stove to see whether they might make less smoke! Madame Marclay excitedly met us, showing us the pile of evergreen branches and trees ready for us to decorate, and assuring us that she would be back with some "four o'clock" (a pail of tea, a loaf of bread, some butter and jam), and hastened us on our way to a tea-room where we had some lunch before beginning the afternoon's work of preparing the logs with candles, placing the greenery around, and so on.

By five o'clock the church was trimmed, the smoke almost all gone, and the fire burning without making much impression on the cold air, though the candle flames gave an illusion of warmth. Karl Woodson stood at the back to hand out hymn sheets, Debby and Dot lighted candles, and Priscilla sat ready to play the pump organ as people began filing in. It was an emotional time for us to see once again the English high school age young people coming in groups, teachers with them, some families coming as units, and some French-speaking people scattered among them. By the time the last person came in during the first carol, there were 175 people there. We felt strongly that it was like seeing a miracle.

Christmas Day we were able to have our traditional family gift opening beside a blazing fire in the new grey stone fireplace, with Susan enthroned on a couch, which was almost as good as being "up", and Franky making enthusiastic remarks about everything, from toys to overalls, as he opened gifts. "That's *just* what I needed."

Karl felt one gift he could give in his time there would be a change from the inactivity he was finding so boring in the Army, and that was the painting of the drab, dirty tan of the kitchen into a clean, sunny yellow and white. He even worked all night one night to finish before his leave was over!

One blustery evening in January the doorbell rang, and when we opened the door, along with a blast of cold wind, in came two strangers who said they had been sent by a young Swiss Christian who knew us. It turned out that they were both teachers in the same boarding school in Villars, and that they had commenced a Bible class on Tuesday evenings in the apartment of one of them. They were asking us to attend, and Fran to help with the teaching. The third teacher, who attended the class although at that time he was agnostic himself, asked if he might bring pupils from the school, down to our living-room one afternoon a week to receive Bible teaching.

As the weeks went on, there were times when we really didn't have enough blankets to go around, or hot-water bottles to take the icy chill away, but somehow we managed with coats put on top of the sparse number of blankets. Those who slept in the living-room had the benefit of the heat that had come from the fireplace throughout the long evening discussions! The absolute wonder was that with only seven beds to put people in at that time, plus the mattresses or couches in the living-room, there seemed to be a "control" of the numbers arriving, so that without any human scheduling it was always possible to care for the number who came, even though it became complicated, as well as hard work, at times. We began praying for more space by the time we had been there nine months!

About four-thirty one early February Saturday the telephone rang. "Hello, this is Dot. Listen, we have a couple of ski casualties. I'm calling from Dr. Clerc's office." My heart sank. "It's Sophie and Manuel. Sophie broke her leg, and almost at the same time Manuel twisted some ligaments or something. I'm here at the doctor's where Sophie is getting her leg put in a cast, and Manuel is having electric treatment. We'll be home in an ambulance soon."

We hurried to fill hot-water bottles for two beds—the bed in the little single room for Sophie, and the one in the four-bed bedroom for Manuel (who was in with John and Bruce). Soon the ambulance driver, Fran and Dot were bringing Sophie in, her leg in a big bulky cast which needed propping up on an ironing board tilted up from bed-level at her hip, to the height of a table at the foot of the bed. This was my first experience of learning how to nurse a patient with a broken leg . . . and Dorothy and I shared the honours as nurse that week!

Dr. Clerc arrived daily to look at his patients, and to give Manuel an electric treatment with a very awe-inspiring machine. Franky was overjoyed to have a chance to be "Assistant" to the doctor on his rounds! We felt God had some special reason for keeping these two at *L'Abri* in this unusual way, and prayed that although Sophie was disappointed that this meant she could not be presented to the Queen of England on the date set for that important event in her life, she might some day see the disappointment as having had a very special meaning in her life.

Manuel was a Portuguese university student, an aristocrat with wavy brown hair, a long wavy brown beard (meticulously trimmed), big brown eyes and beetling dark brows.

Franky whispered when he first saw him, "Mommy, is he 'Manuel in the lion's den'?"—thinking he was the Old Testament character.

This was his third weekend at the chalet, where he had heard something that had caused him to write in the guest book, "I hope to find resolution and clarity to my problems while sailing in this desperation and intranquillity." We prayed for him too, that this unexpectedly longer stay might be something for which he would later be thankful.

It was a strange church service the next morning, as we

placed chairs in the upstairs hall, and two in each bedroom, so that the patients in bed could attend the service! Fran stood in the hall and preached as usual, though there were tantalising odours coming from the kitchen oven nearby, which made it hard to keep Franky still! The results of that service showed that the setting is not the important thing. Anything further from stained glass windows and soft organ music could not be imagined, yet two people came to a clear understanding of the Bible's central message of how to become "born" into the family of God, and Bruce and Anne (two teenagers from a boarding school in Geneva) separately sought out Fran and talked with him about this.

Two days later Anne telephoned from Geneva saying, "Bruce and I want to know whether Mr. Schaeffer can come to Geneva on Thursday afternoon. We only have eight others from the school, but those eight want to ask a lot of questions and we thought we could meet at a tea-room and ask questions."

In two days these "new born" Christians had *only* interested eight others! How many Christians have a reality that bubbles over with excitement so that others are intensely curious to find out what the thrilling news is!

The phone rang another day that week. "Eileen wants to speak to you, Mummy," Debby said.

I went to the phone. "Mrs. Schaeffer, do you remember a young English doctor who came to see you in Champéry last February one evening? She is here again now, and I told her that you have a place in Huémoz where people come for spiritual help; is it all right if she comes?"

In a moment's time Jennifer herself was on the phone. "Are you sure it's all right for me to come?" she said, with a lift in her voice which so vividly reminded me of her wide-apart, brown eyes, her light hair brushed away from her face, her fresh little-girl look. I remembered her straight, graceful walk, and her quick ways.

Back with the others again I said, "Remember that lovely English doctor we all thought looked like a teenager last year in Champéry? Well, she's coming here tomorrow, and she has just left hospital after having polio."

In addition to affected leg muscles, Jennifer's back had been affected, and also her right hand. A lovely bird, and beautiful... but with a broken wing: that was in my mind as I watched Jennifer struggle to make her right hand do the things she wanted to do to help. What about the delicate work her hand had been doing in the accident ward on head injuries; for she had been a surgeon?

"You see, when I look for a job, I'll have to find something quite different—in the medical line—that can be done from nine to five."

Jennifer had been a "liberal" by choice. Intelligent, with a wide knowledge upon which she had based her choice, it did not seem that she would easily come to any great change which would bring her to a position of accepting the Bible's teaching for what it is. The breakthrough of understanding seemed to come when she was talking by the fire one night and suddenly said, "I've got to admit, when I watch a person die—I know something has gone." We ourselves felt as though we were standing on the sidelines watching a supernatural work, the work of the Holy Spirit, as she came to deep conviction that the Bible *is* truth, and as simply as a child accepted what Christ had done for her.

Her first big answer to prayer was a job: teaching anatomy at Oxford University. As she put her life in God's hand, she found He used her there in Oxford, and later in her own home in England, where she and her writer husband Tim and their two little children have a Christian home which is having a real impact on their social circle. Polio may paralyse muscles and change one's former plans, but it cannot paralyse God's purpose for the lives of His children.

Overlapping visits, so many opening new "doors" among widely differing types of people: could it be possible that we had just come to February 14th again? The anniversary of that day we had been told we had to leave Switzerland . . . twelve months before.

CHAPTER FIFTEEN

God sends His Choice of People

THIS WAS still the first year of the experiment—or demonstration—of what would happen if we prayed that God would bring the people of His choice, keep others away, send in the needed financial means to care for us all, and open His plan to us. Of course, I cannot list all the people who came, and tell you what happened to each one. But I want you to get some feeling of what really did take place.

There was Sandy, who at first glance might seem just a chattery dizzy little blonde . . . but who really is a "brain". She began to join us for weekends, came to believe, and brought such a variety of people they sounded like the United Nations when listed!

There was Murray, whom we couldn't talk about without calling him "good old Murray". He was the son of a brilliant psychiatrist, with a fine mind himself, and headed for the same profession. He once exclaimed, "What a switch, what a switch. Most students come to Europe with some sort of faith, and go back existentialists. Me, I came with no faith and go back a Bible-believing Christian. . . . What a switch!"

There was Liselotte, a Swiss secretary, boarding in the same *pension* as John, who found she could come to the café discussion group during her lunch hour. She sat by the fireplace one night and said, "Oh I see it *now*. . . ." She did, too, and believed.

There was Roger, from that same boarding school in Geneva, from a Christian Scientist background, who cried out as excitedly as an explorer finding a new country, "Oh, I understand it all. It fits together like a jigsaw puzzle. Why, it's wonderful!"

There was Barbara, who sat with a strange smile on her face as Franky glimpsed a nicely iced cake coming in for dessert and cried out, "Let's sing 'Happy Birthday' to someone for that cake" . . . and then glancing around the table added, "Let's sing it to Barbara." After the song had died down, Barbara said, "Franky's not so far off. It is a kind of birthday, because I just finished my struggle over believing, and I have accepted Christ as my Saviour. I was born again today."

There was a Norwegian, Helen, who had been known as the sceptic in her circle. She wondered what would happen when she went back to argue for Christianity instead of against all religion.

There was atheistic Justine from Holland, who declared she could never believe, and who later came to an assurance that Christianity was truth.

All this and much more, was taking place during the month of March 1956. A month that had been so dramatic and so uncertain the year before.

Life wasn't easy by any means. There seemed to be constant stacks of dishes to wash, a tremendous succession of meals to prepare, endless sheets to hang out, countless letters to write, hours on end of conversation which took precedence over all other work—because these were people sent to us for a purpose.

Anyone who might be tempted to say, "Great stuff praying for money. Guess I'll stop working and pray"—don't bother even joking about it! Just remember that we prayed for only enough for food and shelter and the bare necessities of life, and our "working hours" were not according to any "union rules"! It hasn't been, nor is it, a life of any kind of "ease", but it has been tremendously exciting to see the reality of communication with God, and to see the reality of His replies, His answers, in the realm of material things, and in the realm of the minds and hearts of human beings.

By the first of April, we had been in the chalet a year, but we had not finished the first year of being *L'Abri*. The next events still belong in the first year.

A telegram signed simply "Jane" informed us that two friends of a missionary named Georgia, in Italy, would be arriving to stay over Easter weekend.

When Debby and I stepped into the house on Saturday afternoon after marketing in Villars the fog crept in with us, but before we could shut the door Priscilla had whispered loudly, "They're here . . . and guess what? They're not some kind of gospel singers, they're opera singers. Go on down and meet them."

Tall, impressive Jane, a dramatic soprano with a good-natured, hearty enthusiasm about many, many things, sat by the fireplace warming herself. "This is Anita," she said, pointing to a tiny, tiny person. "She's a coloratura soprano, studying voice in Milan."

Jane later said she had thought this was a kind of religious hotel, and that she could go to "the meetings" or not, as she chose. As she really was seeking answers to life, she had come, but with the thought that she could escape if she was bored. But she found herself in the midst of a family, not an institution, and there was no escape!

Fran talked to them while I was cooking that afternoon, and after an hilarious dinner during which Jane related many of her amusing experiences in opera, I sat by the fire telling the whole story of our being put out of Switzerland, the miracle of our being provided with this chalet, and the beginning of *L'Abri*.

Jane's energy and interest knew no bounds. She helped wash dishes, read to Franky, talked to bed-ridden Susan, enthused over the village, "loved" the smell of manure, raved about the woods. Her optimism had evidently made her feel that all religions were good, and that the world was really on its way to getting better. However, she listened with increasing soberness to the teaching of Jesus. "I am *the* door . . . I am the way, the truth and the life, no man cometh to the Father but by me."

Jane and Anita were going to leave Monday afternoon, but Jane went for a walk with Fran to talk things over and something happened on that walk to make her put aside her plans to go back until the next day. We did not know what had happened to Jane until we received a letter from Milan a few days later. I will quote part of it:

"When I was in Huémoz I felt perhaps the altitude had affected me, and I wanted to wait until I came back to Milan to find out whether I still felt the same way. You must have been somewhat taken aback when you received my telegram on Wednesday, but not nearly so amazed as myself! When Georgia spoke of you in our Bible class and mentioned a possibility of a visit, I was the least interested, and later said quite flatly that I'd never find the time for such a thing. Now I am perfectly certain that I was led to *L'Abri* by a power quite outside myself, which now I am able to believe was the Holy Spirit, leading me forward in God's plan for my life. Just as it was right that I miss the bus and have the remaining hours necessary for me to accept Jesus Christ as my Saviour. Indeed, I feel that the power of Christ's Spirit has opened my blinded eyes to the true light."

Overlapping Jane and Anita's visit was the arrival of John for two weeks of Bible study during his Easter vacation. He was just in time to help pull up the old linoleum from the hall and scrape the floor in preparation for the new to be put down the next day! That was an evening of "comedy", as we had to put the iron wood stove (to provide heat) from the hall into Dorothy's room, a cabinet into the bathroom, and walk on boards stretched from doorsill to doorsill. Bill, Irv, and "little Bill" arrived from the Army base in Baumholder the next day, and that was the day Jane and Anita missed the bus, so we had to shift Dot upstairs to room with Priscilla, and put Jane and Anita in the double-decker beds in Dot's room, and the four boys in the four-bed bedroom. As the boys had all already become Christians, Fran started a definite Bible study, which took up the mornings, seated around the table on the balcony breakfast nook, and their afternoons were spent in digging the vegetable gardens, turning in the manure, raking and cleaning up the grass and chopping up old branches for firewood.

This Bible-study-gardening time lasted for three weeks, but with a turn-over of students. We wouldn't have had room for all sixteen at once, and we were amazed how the "timing" worked out, without our planning.

May commenced with the chalet being filled with southern drawls and the sound of a male trio as three G.I.s came to ask questions: Paul from Tennessee, Jim from Mississippi, and Jim from Georgia. Before they left, Analie, the very first girl to become a Christian back in Chalet des Frênes that first winter in Champéry, came to spend some time for spiritual refreshment. We had been corresponding with her for six years as she went from South America to Texas, to California, to Germany in succession, and was about to go to Colombia, in airline jobs.

It thrilled us to have *L'Abri* being a tie-up with those who had been helped before, as well as being a place where absolute strangers were being brought in such different ways.

Betty Carlson thrilled with us over all that had happened since she had left Champéry in November of '54, as she stopped for a brief visit during a tour of Europe with a deaf artist and her sister. We had to say good-bye to her, and to the others gathered there that weekend, as Fran and I left for Rome where we had to change trains for a coastal spot, at which he was to be a conference speaker. On our way home from that conference we stopped in Milan, to be present for an evening at Georgia and Maria Theresa's apartment where more than twenty people were gathered to hear a message from Fran on the philosophies and religions of the world, and the Bible's answers to the questions they did not answer. The people were opera singers, artists, musicians, assorted types from assorted countries. Jane stayed long after the others left, telling of all that had been happening in her life, and of her conversations with others in the theatre world concerning the reality of God.

That very weekend Jane came to the chalet again bringing an artist friend, married to a top journalist, to whom success, money and fame had brought only cynicism, not satisfaction.

The following weekend Anita returned, with an English opera singer, John, who argued from a strong atheist's viewpoint, Dino, an Italian building contractor, and Lorna his English wife.

Yes, there were lots of other people both those weekends . . . but I am following a particular thread to bring you to the beginning of a new portion of the *L'Abri* work, which also began before the first year of existence as *L'Abri* was over.

Both Jane, and Anita, had so many contacts in Milan, people who could not come to the chalet, but who wanted to ask questions and discuss, that they asked Fran to come to Milan and lead a discussion group. Thus it was that such a group commenced, first in the apartment of the two girls, Georgia and Maria Theresa, who had already been having regular Bible classes, and then, when they left Milan, in a neutral place, where theatrical people and a variety of non-religious people would not mind dropping in.

That was the beginning of the Milan discussion group, which continued every two weeks with a tremendous succession of people coming both to the hotel where they now met, and to the chalet, though, as many were of various nationalities and only studying there, they did not become a permanent sort of group. However there gradually grew up a small nucleus of believing people.

The first day of the new year, 1959, three years after we began to go to Milan for discussion groups, Dot and Hurvey (whose wedding was described earlier) began a new phase in their lives and *L'Abri* began a new phase of its work.

With a pile of luggage and boxes, topped by a "surprise picnic lunch" for their New Year's dinner on the train, Hurvey and Dot waited for the yellow bus, with all of us there to wave them off. They were on their way to Milan, without any apartment to go into, feeling a bit apprehensive about the length of time they might have to "house hunt". The next morning the phone rang. It was Hurvey giving us the exciting news of another big answer to prayer.

"The impossible has happened again, and we found an apartment, furnished and well located—the very first one we looked at. Dino said it couldn't be found, and now we have actually signed for it."

We felt it to be a clear answer as to the rightness of their going to Italy. They began by studying Italian, having people in for tea and discussions, and having a little Sunday morning service.

The *L'Abri* work in Milan has grown and continued, with a weekend place on a lake being rented for part of the year, for longer times of study and discussion. We have "Italian weekends" at the chalet too, when Hurvey brings up a group, and Dot comes too, or stays down behind to take care of the two little additions, David and his baby sister Anne.

The living-room, Chalet les Mélèzes

CHAPTER SIXTEEN

The Chalet grows

THAT FIRST year really came to an end in June. We have never kept statistics, but I jotted down in a letter that summer that during the six weeks of mid-June to the end of July we had had 187 different guests to stay varying lengths of time. That was the summer that I usually watered the garden at midnight, and sometimes transplanted by flashlight, as the discussion was going on. Jennifer came as a Worker, and insisted that she could "keep up" in spite of her handicap—she was improving tremendously—while Dot travelled with her mother.

When it was time for Jennifer to go Franky wailed, "I've got a scratch! Who's going to fix me now that Doctor Jennifer's gone? Bring her back." We would all have liked her to come back.

The day after Jennifer left, a Dutch art critic and his wife and children arrived. They desired spiritual help, and the only way they could come at that time was to bring the children along, too—ages six, three and two. Dr. Rookmaaker was able to give lectures on Modern Art and Christianity which were helpful to the guests, and he and his wife in their turn gained a new insight into truth—so new, and so profound a change that it became a turning point in their lives. Our contact with them was to bring more than any of us dreamed of in the future of *L'Abri* work.

It was because of the Rookmaakers that Alida Meester came to be a Worker. Alida in turn enthusiastically talked to other Dutch young people when she went home on a vacation. Some other Dutch fellows and girls came, and the Rookmaakers sent still others. Then the Rookmaakers started a discussion group in their home. He was an instructor in Art History at the University of Leiden as well as a critic.[1]

As time went on he urged Fran to come to Holland for a time of discussion with his group, feeling it would be a help to them. When Fran and I were able to make this trip several things happened. Fran had not only time with Dr. Rookmaaker's group, but with other gatherings, particularly at one place in Amsterdam, a furniture store, where the owner Mr. van der Weyden gathered all sorts of Dutch university students and other interested people. Questions and answers continued till after midnight.

These Dutch trips became a regular thing, once or twice a year. The Meesters had us in their home for discussion groups, and when Alida left *L'Abri* to be married to Karl and live in America, the Meesters' daughter Marry took her place (until she had to leave because of illness). The Rookmaakers became *L'Abri* representatives in Holland, and Coxy, a Dutch girl who became a Christian in the Rookmaakers' home, also became a Worker. Dutch fellows began to come to help with gardening in the summer, and some of them began to meet together in Amsterdam to do Bible study in the winter.

Many things sprang from those weeks when it seemed as though it was almost too much to add a whole family, like the Rookmaakers, in the small quarters of one house where such a stream of people was coming and going.

Sometimes when difficult times are being lived through it seems as though the difficulties are simply too mundane to be the least bit worthwhile. Martyrs being tortured or persecuted for their faith at least sounds dramatic. Having to cook, serve meals to two sittings at times without ever sitting down to eat in between yourself, having constantly to clean up spilled and broken things, to empty mounds of garbage, and to scrub a

[1] He is now Professor of Art History at the Free University of Amsterdam.

stove that things have boiled over on, or an oven in which things have spilled over and baked to a black crust is neither dramatic nor glamorous! For the ones who were leading discussions or answering questions or teaching, *L'Abri* had no set hours which had a beginning and ending time, and so often a sigh of relief, and a relaxing with a cup of tea, has been immediately broken into with the arrival of a new person, or batch of persons, who needed to be cared for. The Lord was sending people and amazing things were "springing forth", but the prayer answers brought with them the need to be willing to accept *all* that the answers meant, in the way of work, as well as excitement.

People often say they want to "experience reality", or to "experience contact with God, or with the supernatural". People are even taking drugs to experience an "Experience" these days, wildly searching for some contact with the supernatural; some hoping for a sense of meaning, of "oneness with the universe". What they want is something that can be "turned on" and felt, looked back on and remembered. But they also want a lot of freedom in the use of their lives, as far as rest, recreation and work goes. Most people want their ventures to be limited to nine to twelve on Sundays, or eight to ten on Wednesday nights, or during a two-week period which they choose. This is so, whether it is an exotic "chemical experience" they are seeking, or some religious satisfaction.

What has all this to do with my story? Only this. There are some who are not Christians who would like some sort of a supernatural experience, including the excitement of contacting God, if He exists. But they are *not* willing to examine the evidence and come to Him in the way He has appointed.

There are others who are Christians, who really almost envy the answers to prayer that they hear about, but they want specific answers to some specific requests without the rest of their lives being changed in any way. They would like *some* prayers answered in *some* realms, and they would like to know what it is like to be "led" by God's direction in certain aspects of their lives. They may even present two alternatives to God in their prayers, but they push the rest of the possibilities away.

We are very conscious of this, because the inward battle to be honest before God when one asks "show me Thy will" is a very real struggle. It is so easy to clutch to oneself certain things which really erase the whole request, and annul it. This is not only true at a time of crisis, but is true at any time one asks to be shown *God*'s plan. Many Christians want the excitement of a reply from God, but not the pain of the struggle.

I put this in because it would be a totally unfair picture to go on relating incidents of answered prayer without a constant reminder that much is involved. The whole person is involved in being a Christian. The whole life is involved in living in contact with God. But real life is involved, and the whole of eternity is involved in your conclusions and decisions concerning these things in this life.

We prayed about the chalet on the back road, from which we had been given the library, but although we felt we needed the extra space, when the deadline date arrived we had not the money to begin to buy it. Hence it was sold to other people.

The sun was streaming into the cobblestone patio on the west side of Chalet les Mélèzes one afternoon when Fran and I were walking around thinking of the need of extra sleeping space. "If that patio were enclosed, you could put a double decker bed in there," Fran said.

"Maybe there'd be room for a sort of built-in daybed at one end, too," I added. "It would be more like a ship's cabin than a room, but let's measure the space."

Fran ran off to get a piece of chalk and the measuring tape along with some big pieces of wrapping paper. Soon the floor was marked off into "space for the bed", and "allowance for door into what would be the hall". The paper was cut into "windows" which Lydia and Debby obligingly held in place while we squinted from across the garden. "It won't hurt the looks of the house, in fact, it might add to them." And so the idea took shape of adding three more beds to the chalet. Not long after that Mr. Dubi came to give an estimate of what this new room would cost. He brought a mason with him, who would be laying the foundation, cementing block walls, making a flagstone terrace (to replace the patio, giving a place for serving outdoor meals) and so on.

A letter came during those days from a member of the "Praying Family" who had already given a gift "for providing more space for *L'Abri*". The essence of the letter was that while praying a thought had come to her that a room might be added to Chalet les Mélèzes, until the time came to increase the capacity in another way. We felt this was a sign from God that the room was His plan.

We had enough money to make the foundation and walls for the room, but not to do the flagstone and other things. We ordered what we could pay for, and the mason said he would begin on October 8th. During our vacation in September we prayed very especially that money would come in to finish the room, furnish it, make the flagstone terrace, walk, and steps to the house, and provide blankets and hot-water bottles enough to keep twenty people warm at one time. We prayed that it would be ready for "this winter, if it be Thy will, Lord".

M. Bratschi, the mason, and his helper were hard at work on the frosty morning of October 8th. Franky had a delightful time digging in the piles of dirt which were thrown up as the foundation work began.

"Mr. Schaeffer," the boss said late the next afternoon, "if I can order all the stone for the whole job at one time, I can get a reduced price. Have you decided yet?"

We explained to him that *L'Abri* prayed to God for the provision of all its needs, and that we could only order material when money had come, as we never borrowed against future possibilities of money coming. At present there was enough for the foundation and room. The stone for the terrace and walk could wait.

"But, Monsieur," he replied, "if freezing weather continues the work outside will have to be put off until spring, and in a few days now I must go on to another outside job, unless you want the whole job done *now*."

"We will pray about it, and let you know in a short time," was all we could promise.

We had a day of prayer the next day. Our "Day of Prayer"

was a regular occurrence at *L'Abri*. When I say we "prayed about it" in referring to various parts of the work, or our lives, perhaps you picture a five-minute time of prayer at bedtime. This is not the sort of prayer we are talking about. We feel that if one is talking to the living God who is there, and who receives us into His presence to listen to us, it is worth far more than any other one thing we could do—although there is more involved than just a large amount of time.

Our days of prayer at that time were arranged by placing a chart on the kitchen wall with the hours of the day divided into half-hour periods. There was a place for initials to be written in beside any half-hour spaces each individual wanted to "take". A room was assigned as a prayer room. A list with Bible verses for meditation, and specific prayer requests, was placed in that room, to help the person praying to prepare for prayer and remember what we all were especially agreeing to ask for that particular day. Each person prayed in his own words, however, as the list was only a reminder, not a prayer to be repeated or read. We all felt these days were helpful to us personally, as well as bringing answers to our united requests. It was good to have uninterrupted time for communication with God. We were not interrupted because we were supposed to check the "prayer list" if we couldn't find someone on the day of prayer! This particular day the verse on the chart in the kitchen, which Susan had selected and printed, was this: "Ah Lord God! behold, thou hast made the heaven and the earth by thy great power and stretched out arm, and there is nothing too hard for thee," which comes from Jeremiah 32:17.

When Alice came with the mail, Dot was in the prayer room, but everyone else rushed to the front door with a feeling of expectancy. Fran began to read one letter, and then gave a general call. . . .

"Come to the dining-room everyone, we have something to tell you."

A scraping of chairs, a hush, and everyone waited. Our family, Lydia, Dot, Hurvey, two English R.A.F. boys and Alice . . . Fran explained a bit of the background of our need for the new room, and then asked me to read the letter. It was from someone who said that several weeks before she had had a great desire to send a gift to enlarge *L'Abri*, as she had been there herself, and felt the need acutely. She had expected some money from an estate, with which to make this gift, but it became increasingly clear that this was not going to come for a long time. Finally she said she felt such an urgency that she had telephoned a lawyer long distance, and had asked for a sum for this purpose immediately. The request was granted, and the sum was enclosed!

It meant that we could go outside and tell the workman, "Go ahead and order the stone, go ahead and finish the job."

We were all silent with awe for a moment, then Franky broke the silence with, "You know what *I* think we should do about this? I think we should all *clap*!" So Franky led us in clapping our thanks to the Living God, the praise a little four-year-old could understand and mean in a very real way. The day of prayer continued as a special thanksgiving time!

In the first winter we had the living-room and fireplace, and by the second winter we had the new room and other improvements including blankets and hot-water bottles. All during this time the day-by-day needs had been met. Often we had to economise and make food "stretch" with recipes which used little meat, yet served a lot of people with an appetising meal, often we had to go without certain personal things, but never was there an unpaid bill, and never was anyone turned away because we had nothing left to share!

We needed all the space we had that winter, as more were coming from Lausanne, Milan and Basle. Jewish medical students became interested, and we had a number of brilliant atheistic ones arguing vehemently. Poor Franky one evening was sitting on Jay's lap as Jay became agitated in a debate and used Franky to emphasise points by bouncing him up and down! There were more singers coming from Milan, and one weekend Claudie, a singer from California, and Doris, a singer from New York, both became Christians, one after the other. Two Jewish girls from the University of Lausanne became Christians, feeling "proud of being Jewish" for the first time in their lives, they said, because of the wonder of the Bible's teaching, showing the unbroken "stream" of believers from Abraham on, who were either looking for the Messiah, or accepting Him when He was on earth, or believing the records of Him given in the Bible.

Greek Anna, an intellectual philosophy student, came to us in an amazing way, during a moment of extreme need, and stayed three months with us, until her nameless baby was born, and she went back to another country to finish her studies in the university there. She went back, however, as a believing Christian.

Swiss Fritz, who had become an atheist studying under neo-orthodox theologians in Basle and Zürich, and had changed from theology to pedagogy, came to find out what in the world a man who believed the Bible to be verbally true could ever have to say. Fritz became a Christian, and is today (six years later) a pastor in Switzerland preaching the Bible from the viewpoint of its being true. His wife was an agnostic German refugee from East Germany, who found her way to *L'Abri* the summer Fran and I were away . . . and was brought to an understanding and belief through the handful of young people carrying on in our absence. Ina and Fritz met at *L'Abri*.

That second winter a small Bible class commenced in the home of a ski teacher in Champéry, and Fran went over once every two weeks. As March came around again, a Swiss girl, Claudie, came to *L'Abri* because of contacts she had made in America while there as an exchange student. Her coming to an understanding belief was another "important thread" in the future, as she begged Fran to come to Montreux and talk to her friends. That was the beginning of the Montreux Bible class, which began with her friends, and later changed in character as she left for college in America, and her parents became interested, and invited their friends.

Dot and Hurvey were married that May and left for America, which left us praying for the Lord's choice of people to take their places. Almost immediately a temporary Worker came named Jo Harper, a girl travelling through Europe and feeling "led" to come and help for a time. Then the owners of Beau

Site, the house next door to Les Mélèzes on the other side, died, and the two brothers decided to let it, as the Mademoiselles Chaudet had found a chalet in the village they wanted to buy, and were moving. A letter came to us from a mother who had just been widowed, and wanted to come to be near *L'Abri* for the summer, which seemed to indicate renting Beau Site for them. No sooner had we looked into the arrangements for this, than a letter came from Jim and Joyce Hughes asking to be *L'Abri* Workers. So when the Williams family and Mrs. Caldwell left after spending the summer in Beau Site, the Hughes moved in with their two small boys, and *L'Abri* started its third winter with two houses, and more beds for guests! At that time only half of Beau Site was rented, as it was divided into two apartments, which gave us only six extra beds: but that was a considerable gain, all the same.

A view from Huémoz

CHAPTER SEVENTEEN

Life goes on
in the Midst of L'Abri

THAT THIRD autumn, Fran had another class to teach which required five hours of travel going and coming. It was in Basle, where Anne, Mary and Rosemary had a number who wanted to have a regular class and discussion group, some from the hospital, and some from the university. But there was one person who sat in those classes with intent interest, taking avid notes. She is yet another "thread" to another whole section in this tapestry of *L'Abri*.

It was a July weekend when Hilary arrived, with Rosemary and a Danish therapist. The circle around the hot dog roast numbered twenty-five, which meant it was a "big weekend". After the Sunday morning church service, and dinner in the dining-room (with an overflow sitting on the balcony beside an open window so that they could get in on the conversation), and after dishes had been finished with the help of a crowd in the kitchen, Fran took a group for a walk, and Hilary asked if she could talk to me. To make this possible, Susan and Lydia took charge of getting tea ready, making it possible for me to go upstairs, shut a door, and forget about everything but Hilary for a couple of hours.

With our feet curled up on the couch, Hilary looked at me with her direct, dark blue eyes full of hope, and after relating something of her Jewish background, the Ethical Society teaching, her time as a concert violinist and her vain search in the medical field for satisfaction in helping humanity, she said, "Now how can I be sure that I really believe? That I am sincere in accepting this as truth? What must I do to become a Christian? Mr. Schaeffer made things so clear in his sermon this morning, but I want to know how it can become personal to *me*."

"Look Hilary, we have something we call 'The four questions'. They really aren't just four questions but four *areas* in which a person can measure himself to judge where he stands, in the matter of becoming a Christian. I think it might help to begin with these areas, and then go on from there, if you have anything else that is bothering you.

"The first one would be, *do you believe God exists*? A person cannot become a Christian without believing truly in the existence of God, believing that He is *there*. In this day of terminology being used to mean a variety of different things, often quite opposite from each other, it is important to be certain that a person understands that the Bible states that there is a Personal, Infinite, Holy, Just, Loving God, who is three persons, Father, Son, and Holy Spirit. That these three persons have always existed, without a beginning, have always had communication within the Trinity and have always loved each other—and that this gives us the explanation of personality in the universe. Love and communication was a reality in the Trinity before the creation.

"The Bible teaches that this God created the universe, and that He created man 'in his own image' . . . that is, as a personality who could think, feel, and have valid choice. Of course, Hilary, it would take a long time to make an exhaustive study of the God of the Bible, but when we say you must believe in the existence of God, it is the *God of the Bible* we are talking about, not the God of some human being's definition: whether defined in wood, stone and gold as a material image, or defined in words as an image of the imagination.

"The second one would be, *do you acknowledge the fact that you are a sinner*, and realise that you cannot get rid of the guilt of this sin by yourself? The whole question of what sin is, is involved here; and no one can *perfectly* feel or realise his own sinfulness in the light of how God would see it. We can only have a measure of understanding of our own guilt. Some feel great heaviness, others are not able even to feel much reality in this realm, but there must be *some* understanding of the fact that we have not even kept our *own* standards perfectly, let alone God's perfect standard. We must understand to some degree the fact that we are guilty of sin in the presence of a Holy God, and that it is not just a matter of psychological 'guilt feelings' resulting from our mothers doing the wrong thing to us when we were babies, but that it is true moral guilt. It is coming to understand something of what the Bible means in this area, that brings us to a realisation of our need of finding a way to get rid of this sin."

Hilary kept nodding her head through these two, and said, "Oh, I have no problem in each of those first two questions. I really do think I can honestly say I believe God exists, and I have no trouble at all *knowing* I have sinned, and am sinful. It is so obvious that one cannot keep the ideals and standards one sets up for oneself even. Yes, I can really say 'yes' to those two."

"Then the third one would be, *do you believe that Jesus came, in space, time and history*, to be born of a virgin, to live the sinless life recounted in the New Testament; that He died on the cross for the sins of men, to take their place as a substitute receiving their deserved punishment; that He rose again on the third day, also in space, time and history; that He then really spoke a command to His followers to tell the world about Him, and then ascended into heaven, from which place we are told He will some day come back again. Do you believe that all this took place in history and that when He died His substitutionary work was completely accomplished? This is the third area."

Again Hilary assented, and said, "All this is certain to me now, but . . ."

"It's true that a person can believe these first three 'areas' of fact with his intellect, and yet not really be a Christian. The fourth question or area involves *bowing to this God, and accepting what Christ did as for you, personally and individually, taking your deserved punishment, for your individual sins, as He died outside Jerusalem.*

"Let me give you an illustration that might help to clarify what the word 'personally' means in this context. There is one thing I do for a lot of people, and that is, cook. It happens that as I am cooking there in the Mélèzes kitchen, I never have the feeling that it is for a mass of unknown people. I do it for individuals. I remember that Deane loves Macedonian stew and give him an extra large portion, that Jeremy hates hot dogs and slip a substitute in his roll, that Trudy is allergic to spinach so fix her a salad of lettuce instead. But that isn't the only sort of thing. I do what I am doing so that those who eat will have the opportunity to have the spiritual food which conversations at mealtimes often provide, and I pray for the people as individuals, with a picture in my memory of their eyes, hair, features—thinking of them as individuals.

"Now I am a finite person, and very, very limited and imperfect. My love is not perfect, nor is it equal for all who come. But, if I, as a finite person, can keep the faces, personalities and needs of a growing number of human beings in my mind, in my prayers and emotions as personalities, and not as a mass, then what about Jesus? Jesus is God. He is infinite. He is not limited. He has perfect love, and perfect understanding—not just for some kinds of people, but for all men. He then was able to die for thousands upon thousands of individuals, not as a mass, but as separate personalities He knows by name. It is in this very real sense, then, that one needs to become conscious of what Jesus did with love for the person who accepts Him as Saviour.

"It's not a matter of grabbing on to a bunch of slogans, nor of having merely an emotional experience, Hilary. It is for good and sufficient reasons *believing* these things are true, and then making a definite decision to accept, and say 'Thank you' to God for it."

I can't relate in detail a two-hour conversation, but we went on looking up some specific passages in the Bible. Hilary was going through a struggle which showed on her face, but which I could not help from the outside. Then suddenly a light broke on her face, and "light" is really the only way to describe it. She prayed softly, aloud, accepting and thanking God. Just two seconds after that it was Debby at the door: "Sorry, Mother, but they have to go" . . . and Hilary threw her arms around me, thanked me, rushed down the stairs, grabbed her things as people held them out to her, dashed out of the front door—and Rosemary, waiting for her, looked back over her shoulder smiling a smile of the happiest understanding, because she suddenly knew what had happened.

Priscilla and John's wedding took place at *L'Abri*—in the beautiful thirteenth-century church, where Farel preached 450 years ago, starting the Reformation in this part of Switzerland. Dr. Martyn Lloyd-Jones of Westminster Chapel, London, preached the sermon on this memorable occasion.

Yes . . . weddings have been "fitted in" at *L'Abri*, but usually, as with this one, by the time the wedding reception is over, the caramels are all thrown out of moving car windows to the waiting Swiss children, the bride and groom farewelled . . . a new discussion is in full swing by evening, as people eat a buffet supper in the living-room.

March began as a "dark" month, with Joyce having mononucleosis, Aly having chronic appendicitis, Franky having bronchitis and Susan suddenly being taken to Aigle hospital for an operation for appendicitis, while John Sandri came down with infectious hepatitis.

Franky remarked to someone who went up to see him . . . "I have appendicitis . . . or no . . . hepatitis . . . oh no, it's *bron*chitis . . . I'm always getting mixed up around here, we have so many things, I can't remember which one of them I have!"

That March brought several other physical "blows". Arnie (a theological student who had come to work in *L'Abri* for a year, expecting to learn much as he listened in to "live discussions") had broken his leg ski-ing. That made another to nurse, as well as a Worker incapacitated. And then Debby went ski-ing on a very warm sunny day, to keep Deirdre company, and came home saying, "The sun felt so good, I know I'm going to have a tan tomorrow," as I exclaimed over the redness of her face. But in the morning Debby's face was swollen twice its normal size, eyes mere slits, and on top of the swollen face were long blisters! In a few minutes I was consulting Joyce's medical books on burns, and Debby was ensconced in bed, needing treatment for shock.

All this . . . and ten people were arriving. Is there a *reality* to God's leading? Certainly the battle seemed real—discouragements were being thrown like buckets of icy water on the inner feelings.

Added to this succession of things was the disheartening arrival of nothing in the mail. There were lots of "printed matter", but few letters, and no cheques. Medical bills were being added to ordinary expenses, and that "icy water" chilled us at times—the icy chill of discouragement designed to make one disappear down the hole of doubt.

We had a regular day of prayer. The following day Jane, who had come in between operas for some days of study, suggested that we have another morning. "I'll take two hours," she said, and soon the other half-hours were all filled up. We agreed to have special prayer for the financial needs of the month—really serious needs by now.

The first letter to arrive was not what we had been praying for at the time, but was a startling one which we recognised as a definite "signpost" for the way ahead. *L'Abri* was going to have a new and unexpected development.

The letter came from Ann Bent, a therapist in an Oxford hospital, who had become a Christian at *L'Abri*. She said she had received a large gift for *L'Abri*, designated for use in England. Hilary had sent it, feeling an urge one day, as she was praying for members of her family, and friends in England, to make it possible for the Schaeffers to go to England, and talk with people in the same informal manner as at *L'Abri*.

"Please put this in the bank," she wrote to Ann, "and use it for air-tickets and hotel rooms, and arrange whatever it is necessary to arrange for the Schaeffers to be in London for a time."

She had sent money which she had saved towards a trip to America, feeling that it was far more important for some in

England to have an opportunity to see the truth than for her to see America!

This was a reply to another time of prayer, one which I had had with Deirdre and Jean, English girls, during which we asked that God might give an opening for us to talk with friends of theirs in London, about whom they were concerned. That prayer-time had taken place a year before.

Lucinda was in the prayer room when the next mail came. None of us will ever forget that long, thin notepaper bordered in blue, and a short little note in precise handwriting, with a cheque clipped to the second page. It was for 500 dollars! We had had almost nothing at all for the month, five minutes before. It came from a person we had not heard from ever before. Later we found that it was a schoolteacher in the Mid-West, who had felt a strong conviction that she should send that amount.

"Oh, isn't that exciting," said Jane. "You know that is the amount I asked for this morning as I prayed."

It *was* exciting, because once more it seemed that God was speaking to us and giving a token of His hearing our prayer. It was an encouragement to go on praying with faith, and waiting for His perfect timing of His answers. By the time March's bills came in, there was sufficient to pay them.

Easter brought more exciting "beginnings". The heavy fog of difficulty had lifted, and we could almost feel the change, as it seemed to us a spiritual struggle had been won, first inwardly, and then with a succession of events which gave evidence to that.

A letter brought the news that Deirdre from London was stopping for two days on her way back from a ski trip with her mother. That meant the coming London trip could be planned without a long exchange of letters. She had no knowledge that we were going to be able to go to London, nor of Hilary's gift, when she planned to stop.

Easter Sunday brought Jeremy Rutland, an English teacher from another boarding school in Chesières, with twelve students between the ages of twelve and seventeen for church, bringing a bunch of daffodils to help make the blizzardy day seem spring-like! This was their first Sunday with us—the first of many, and the beginning of a Bible class for that school. The contact continued as long as Jeremy taught in that school, and beyond —now he is next door at Bellevue, teaching the cerebral palsy children, helping in a multitude of ways in that work and occasionally preaching on Sundays at *L'Abri*.

Wendy had come for a few weekends from Lausanne. She was working in the university towards a French Certificate, and also towards a difficult music composition exam at the Conservatory at the same time: an unheard of thing to attempt! She came up for ten days at Easter. A brilliant girl, she was an atheist, both by choice and tradition, as her family had been atheistic for two generations. That week she came to a certainty that what she was hearing was truth, and found that she was able honestly to say "yes" in all the four areas I spoke of earlier. Wendy begged us to visit her family during our coming English trip, a most significant request, as it turned out.

That same week Marry, Aly's sister, arrived, and it was then that she had her "eyes of understanding" opened. Not that she had not heard the Bible's message before—she had grown up in it; but there is a difference between hearing words, and "spiritual understanding".

That very same week José walked into the garden looking inquiringly up at the chalet, just as the weekend had ended. José was an engineering student at the University of Lausanne, who had won the "first prize" in his country of El Salvador, as the brightest prospect of the whole country that particular year—the prize being seven years of study to prepare him for engineering. He became a strongly convinced Christian after some months . . . and his younger friend, Mario, bounced into our lives!

Mario, the winner of the same prize another year, brightest high school senior in the country, also studying engineering, was the most vivid and enthusiastic personality, reminding us of Tigger in Winnie the Pooh. He really "bounced" over many things, but especially over the excitement of his discoveries in the Bible, as though they were being discovered for the first time by man. It was refreshing to us all. Though he had a long struggle before he came to "see and believe", he is now quite a leading figure in El Salvador, and he writes that his life is very different from what it would have been otherwise.

All of this serves to demonstrate, over a short period of weeks, the tremendous contrasts that we experienced. It seemed as though we lived through testing times, times when it was important to "wait" with trust in God and to pray with faith that He could do the impossible, followed by times when the prayer answers, "signs" and "path markers" flowed in in almost frightening succession.

We could in no way attribute these things to "chance" or "coincidence". We were increasingly sure that our basic desire to have the work used in the twentieth century as a demonstration of God's existence was being answered.

The gateway, L'Abri, London

CHAPTER EIGHTEEN

English L'Abri is born

IT WAS June of 1958 when Fran and I arrived in London, to be met by Deirdre who had a little book with pages dated for the days we would be there, and the rest of the paper blank! She and Ann had decided upon a centrally located hotel near Marble Arch, had arranged for a bedroom and living-room so that we would have space to receive people, and two places to talk (in case personal conversations were needed). People who had been in *L'Abri* from that area, had been informed that we would be there, and non-Christian friends and relatives had been told. Otherwise the girls had simply prayed that the ones of God's choice would choose to come to the hotel rooms, and others would stay away. It was a tiny part of *L'Abri* in the heart of busy, swirling London.

In that week, over seventy-five different people made their way to the hotel suite. Some came several times. Some came in groups so that an evening's discussion and question and answer period was just like that around the fireplace in Mélèzes, minus fireplace, and minus the Alpine atmosphere. Some came alone with personal questions and problems.

One afternoon we were invited to Cambridge, where we were met by Mike, a South African student, and conducted to the living-room of a student at St. Catherine's College where about a dozen were gathered for tea, and to hear a message given by Fran. They came with a sceptical attitude towards this unknown American. But it was to be the first of many times in Cambridge, with many groups of students, particularly men reading science. Among others there that day was Hugh, a complete stranger to us then, but later to be a *L'Abri* Worker for a time, and Ranald, also a stranger to us then, also to be a *L'Abri* Worker and to be our Susan's husband! We knew nothing of this future which commenced that day, as we hurried off to get the train back to London in time for the evening group arriving at the hotel. We had our first glimpse of Cambridge's beautiful courts, the quiet River Cam and fields with placid cows grazing, within sight of the university buildings. It was not until years later that we were to have our first punt trips in Cambridge.

It was during the Christmas holidays that the first group of Cambridge students arrived at *L'Abri*. A postcard had informed us that they would arrive at 3.23 and a half . . . in the afternoon! On the dot an old London taxi, with flowered curtains drawn back from the windows in ridiculous imitation of looped back kitchen curtains, drew to a rattling stop. Out poured a group of laughing young people, to show us proudly that the lights would even go on if you kicked the car in just the right fashion. They were an hilarious group, with a tremendous sense of humour, and personality, and brains! One of them, who was then captain of the polo team, and a good rugby player, as well as a fine student, is now preaching in Africa, in a tiny but excellent mission in South Africa.

But there is no space here to follow "threads" too far away. As far as *L'Abri* is concerned, from that time on Cambridge students, and soon after that Oxford students, and later students from St. Andrews in Scotland, began to come to *L'Abri*, and to have informal discussion groups or question and answer times when we went to England. At one time twenty atheists were gathered to fire questions at Fran for a three-hour period in one of the colleges. Many were the intense intellectual discussions commenced and continued.

Another significant "beginning" took place in Surrey as a Sunday "dinner and the afternoon" invitation to Wendy's home was accepted. We found her home set in apple orchards, with a charming English garden rambling around it, a wee stream widening into a small lily pond, then a larger pond with lush rhododendrons surrounding it. A fenced-in field kept her sister's horse from straying—a story-book horse which had been rescued in a scraggy condition and nursed into health by its loving fifteen-year-old mistress, who loved to study her lessons beside the horse, sharing an apple with him. After dinner we separated into two groups at the ends of the drawing-room, Fran with Wendy's father, and I with her mother and a young ballet dancer in a pale blue knitted dress who had a nervously gay look that kept slipping at the edges to show the lost wistfulness underneath.

"And just what *is* your work in Switzerland?" asked Wendy's mother, either to be polite, or with some sort of an interest.

Whichever it was, she got a three-hour answer, because how could you explain *L'Abri* in ten minutes? I couldn't. I had to start at the beginning and tell the whole story. I couldn't tell what Wendy's mother thought, but Linette's wistfulness filled her eyes. In answer to my question, "where do you live?" Linette answered: "When you come back to London, do let me know. I'd like to come to one of your discussion groups, or classes. Here's my address." And that was the first time we glanced at the address of 59 Sloane Gardens.

Wendy ran out to meet us as we arrived at the Lausanne café straight from the train, in time for the lunch hour discussion group. "Oh, hello. How did you get along in England? And how did you get along in my home? What sort of interest did my parents have?"

"I'm not sure, Wendy, but there was a ballet dancer there, who seemed to be really interested."

"Oh, *Linette* . . . that would be Linette. Oh, I'm *glad* she was there, let me tell you something about her."

What Wendy told me made me go home and write to Linette that very day. We don't usually give special invitations to come to *L'Abri*, but this invitation would have been sent whether there had been a *L'Abri* in existence or not.

"After what Wendy has told me, I feel you need a bit of

home life, peace, joy and quiet before you go on into the next things you need to do."

The response from Linette was immediate: "Your words 'home life, joy, peace', made me long to come. I'll probably be there about the time this letter is."

Susan had rushed to the dinner table excitedly to tell us the news that had just come over the telephone . . . (the Swiss number you dial for news) . . . "American troops are landing in Lebanon . . . perhaps we are going to have another world war!" Details followed and were added to as everyone around the table gave an opinion or an idea sparked by vivid imaginations.

As chairs scraped back, and dishes were carried out to the kitchen, Fran whispered to me as I started to go to the office, "Edith, go out on the balcony to Linette, I think she needs you."

I knew by this time that life seemed purposeless and empty to Linette—at twenty-one. One Sunday after breakfast four years before her father had gone to his room to lie down with a pain in his chest, and had died, of a heart attack. It was a time when Linette was home. She found no source of comfort in the vague things said to her by the local vicar. About two years later, Linette had been with her mother at a party. Her mother went home a bit early, and forty-five minutes later Linette came home to find her mother unconscious. . . . The police found where she had been hoarding sleeping pills from an often renewed prescription. She died three days later without regaining consciousness. The mother's sorrow and desperation had sought oblivion as an escape, blinded at the time to all but her own desire to get away. Linette was left to face the emptiness and aloneness which an only child can share with no one. Is it surprising that a solution to life's basic questions was needed? The *need* is the same for everyone: it is only the realisation of that need that is more acute in some situations where the soft paddings of life are torn away, and the bare skeleton shows through.

Now Linette wept softly on the balcony, head pillowed on her arms as she sat on the breakfast bench, and leaned on the rail.

"I'm afraid . . . and lonely. I can't go through another war . . . alone."

I had a feeling inside of sympathy which had a physical hurt connected with it. Who wouldn't be afraid? Alone in a world filled with rumours of wars, no certainty of life, no assurance of anything after death? How many fearful lonely people are there in the world, who weep in the dark, unseen, feeling that life is chaos, and their feet are on quicksand?

I put my arm around her, and suggested that we go upstairs and talk. The rest of the family understandingly left us alone, and took care of the work to be done, stopping to pray while we were talking.

The thing which Linette felt had made things clear for her, she later told me, was an unplanned talk we had had after breakfast on her first morning at the chalet, when I gave what I call, "the bird's eye view of the Bible". So many people think of the Bible as an unconnected series of stories and never realise the amazing unity of it all.

"Look, Linette," I had said, "Here's a very simple line drawing I often make on a scrap of paper to illustrate the central teaching of the Bible, from beginning to end:

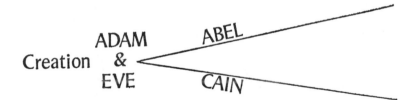

"Adam and Eve talked to God 'in the cool of the day' we are told. They had direct communication with Him, and they were given His teaching by direct word of mouth. He communicated to them; they heard, and accepted what He said with their minds. Whenever anyone speaks to anyone there is an element of believing, or doubting what they say. That isn't very mystical or complicated, it is what takes place constantly. To believe that something is accurate and true, or to doubt it, or believe it is false, is not something that needs to be explained. You don't need to say, 'What do you mean *believe*?' when someone says, 'The water of lake Ontario is icy cold in June. You can get a blistering sunburn on a hot day if you keep going in and out of that icy water and lie in the hot sun in between times.' You either believe that to be true, and a good warning to remember, or you doubt it, and think you'll try it out yourself.

"God told Adam that the fruit of the trees of the whole area they had to live and roam in was theirs to 'freely eat' . . . except for the fruit of one tree. 'The day you eat that, you shall die.' It was real fruit, though of what kind we do not know. The test was one of belief or trust in what God had *said*. Adam and Eve were not troubled as to whether God existed. They knew that. It is no tremendous step to take to believe that a person exists. Are you very pleased if you speak to a child, or anyone over whom you have some authority, and give a statement of fact, coupled with a command, and they say, 'Oh, I believe you exist'?

"No, it was not the *existence* of God that was involved, it was believing what He *said* to be true, or false: to call Him truthful, or a liar.

"When Satan, who had formerly been Lucifer, an angel—in fact, the most beautiful of all the angels, created before man—had revolted against God, because he wanted to be equal with Him and had been cast out of heaven, along with the other angels who rebelled against God, his one great driving purpose was to destroy God's creation.

"His temptation of Eve was in the realm of casting doubts on her simple acceptance of what God had said. 'Hath God said?' he questioned. 'Hath God said . . . ye shall not eat of every tree of the garden?'

"Eve repeated what God had said to them, ending with, 'God hath said, ye shall not eat of it, neither shall ye touch it, lest ye die.' Doubt was already a hideous little seed planted in her mind.

"Satan's comeback to that was a flat denial: 'Ye shall *not* surely die. For God knows that in the day ye eat, then your eyes shall be opened and ye shall be as gods, knowing good and evil.'

"Now it is Satan's word against God's. Satan has accused God of wanting to keep Adam and Eve in ignorance. He dangles the temptation of superior knowledge before her eyes. He tempts Eve with his own desire, to be equal with God.

"Now there is a clear choice. Eve may believe God, in which case she would not eat, because she would not want the result she would then believe to be inevitable. Or she may believe Satan, and eat, to obtain the result she believes to be certain. Eating of the fruit was a direct demonstration of believing Satan rather than God.

"Now we come to Cain and Abel. They would clearly have been instructed by their parents as to how to approach God in worship. For though the result of Adam and Eve's disobedience and unbelief was immediate spiritual death, or separation from God, and the commencement of physical death, in all the abnormalities of the physical world which then came into being, they were never left without a way to come back into communication with God. They were told immediately of One who would be coming, someone who would be born of a woman who would have victory over the 'serpent' or Satan. We also know that they knew something of coming to God with a lamb, used as a sacrifice. Abel brought a lamb. Cain brought vegetables and fruit he had raised, and offered these. Why was Abel's sacrifice acceptable, and Cain's not? It seems to me clear, especially from the rest of the Bible, because it all hangs together. Cain came in defiance, saying something of this sort: 'My fruits are good enough, *I* have raised them. God must accept me because of these very good works I've brought to Him.' Abel came believing what God had said, that the worship must be with a lamb. It was simply believing God, coming in God's way. This is biblical faith.

"That is the very simple difference between these two lines, and if there were time, we could go through the whole Bible and see the exciting tie-up in detail:

"All through the Old Testament communication and worship took place with a lamb being presented. Noah worshipped with a lamb, Abraham brought the lamb, Moses told the children of Israel to prepare the lamb at the time of the passover.

"One night the angel of death was to pass over Egypt striking the firstborn of every family, to force Pharaoh to let the people of Israel go. The Israelite families had to select a perfect lamb, put it aside to see if it developed a blemish, then kill it, take some of the blood, and place it on the door posts. When the angel saw the blood, he would pass over that household and the firstborn would live. At that time it demonstrated belief and trust in God's word through Moses. It also, however, perfectly pictured the One who was coming, whose death would give life—forever.

"All through the Old Testament, however, the lamb was used in looking forward to a future moment, in belief, that someone was coming who would be the Lamb. I have placed an arrow on Abel's line, simply pointing to the cross, indicating that *all* who lived before the coming of Christ, became children of God, in communication with Him, through belief in the coming One. It was the coming death of Christ that cleansed them from sin's guilt before God, and the lambs were only a picture of that which would one day take place.

"Isaiah the Jewish prophet spoke of the One who was coming, in these words: 'He is despised and rejected of men; a man of sorrows, and acquainted with grief: . . . Surely he

179

hath borne our griefs, and carried our sorrows: . . . But he was wounded for our transgressions, he was bruised for our iniquities: . . . he is brought as a lamb to the slaughter, and as a sheep before her shearers is dumb, so he openeth not his mouth: . . . he bare the sin of many, and made intercession for the transgressors.'

"This clear picture of what the promised Messiah was going to do, was written 700 years before He came. This was the One looked forward to in all the references to 'lambs' in the Old Testament.

"And then when Christ was born, the long awaited One, where was the place of His birth? A stable. So perfect for the birth of a *lamb*! The picture was perfectly carried out. John the Baptist called Him 'the lamb' as he cried out, 'Behold the Lamb of God that taketh away the sins of the world!'

"The New Testament in the words of Jesus Himself makes very clear the fact that Christ had come as a fulfilment of all that had been spoken in the Old Testament. 'If ye had believed Moses, ye should have believed me; for he wrote of me.' 'He that believeth on me hath everlasting life.'

"Those who lived during the time Jesus was on the earth had the opportunity of seeing Him, seeing evidences of His being all that He claimed to be. But *the Way* was the same then as before He came; it was a simple matter of believing what God said, and coming to Him in the way He set forth. 'I am *the* way, *the* truth, *the* life, no man cometh unto the Father but by me,' Jesus said. He made it clear that He was the long-awaited 'Lamb of God', promised as far back as the Garden of Eden, believed by Abel and a host of others in the stream of history.

"Now we live in the time after Christ's life and death on the earth. We have the written record which points us to the Cross and Christ's death as having taken place *for* us, in place of our being punished, just as thoroughly as the Jew's lambs were killed that the firstborn of the household could live.

"And in the future? We are told that one day we shall hear names read out of 'The Lamb's Book of Life' . . . a book with the names of those who have believed God: believed what He said, not just that He exists. It is still the 'Lamb' that is used to indicate Christ, the Messiah. And in the last chapter of the Bible we are told that there is in heaven 'a pure river of the water of life, clear as crystal proceeding out of the throne of God, and of the Lamb. . . . And there shall be no more curse: but the throne of God and of the Lamb shall be in it; and they shall see His face. . . .'

"Oh, it all ties together through the centuries, right into eternity. There *is* a way to be in communication with God now, because of 'The Lamb', and we *are* able to have a certainty for the future.

"What about the other line on the little sketch? That one comes from Cain's insistence upon approaching in his own way, devised in his own imagination as a very acceptable way, based on what he had done. I have put many lines branching off that main line. It seems to me a perfect way of quickly picturing the 'many ways to heaven' thought up by man, all of which have one thing in common: the feeling that we can bring some religious or moral good work, some humanistic work, and on that basis be acceptable to God. Examine the ideas of men, and you will find that they do have this common denominator. This, according to the Bible is an evidence of denying the truth of what God has said. Man has been given free choice from the beginning. He is not a puppet, and no one will force him to believe, or act upon anything he does not want to. However, consequences of his belief and actions are set forth. The choice is always his."

This is brief, as far as giving all the wonders of the teaching of the Bible. But it helps to show that it is not a collection of stories and proverbs, but excitingly gives one message through the centuries: not a musty, dry message that has nothing to do with today, but one that provides the facts and the hope that man needs.

It was midnight when Linette said she felt she understood, and believed that what the Bible said was true. I could not see into her mind, I couldn't 'see' sincerity, honesty, the reality of the words she was saying, but I can report what happened. Linette bowed her head, and prayed. She raised her head, and smiled a radiant smile, and said with a kind of breathless astonishment, "Why . . . I'm not afraid any more . . . and I'll *never* be alone again."

Linette stayed for three weeks. She went back to London to dance again for a year. She not only went back to her circle in the theatre, but she also went back to the Surrey village, walked into that country home, and went through the auctioning of furniture and property. Linette, who had said she could not face entering the place, had an inner "something" which made all the difference.

"What's happened to Linette?" old friends and neighbours asked each other. "She looks like a bride, as radiant as . . . well, I've never seen anything like it."

It wasn't a "young man", as some of them wisely shook their heads and supposed it must be, it was a *reality* of communication with God who was now her Father. It was a reality of the Holy Spirit who had entered her, and His presence within her was as visible as the wind in that willow tree I mentioned before. *Something* had happened to Linette all right!

Later, Linette wrote to the chalet, after one production had come to a close—that letter which arrived just as we were praying for someone to take Anne and Mary's place. It said, "Funny . . . but I used to say years ago that I would never give up dancing unless I found someone or something I loved more, never thinking there ever could be anyone or anything. Little did I know! The future is a question mark, but I cannot go on in the theatre." Anne and Mary made their promissory payment on Bellevue the afternoon after the letter arrived, and moved in to await *their* next step. Linette came to the chalet in June, as a Worker.

"About the flat in London," Linette said. (We had been using it instead of a hotel suite after the first English trip, as Linette insisted on its being the "little *L'Abri* of London" from the first, and she would move out for those days.) "I've been thinking, it would be good to have someone live there all the time, in case people want to come for help."

Hilary was in the area at that time, although soon after, she went to Buenos Aires to head up a school of occupational therapy, and Hilary was the first one to live in the flat so that a tiny London *L'Abri* centre began. A succession of *L'Abri* Workers has lived there since. One was a Jewish girl put out of her home for becoming a Christian, who not only found shelter there, but made it a spiritual shelter for others, who came and found talking to Rosalind like coming to a tower of spiritual strength, for the persecutions she had undergone had helped to make her strong.

The flat continued to be used. Sermons, studies, and discussions were taped, and a tape-recorder made it possible for people to gather for an evening, listen for a time to Fran on tape, and then discuss among themselves. When we went to England, the flat was our base, and with some furniture moved out, and every inch of floor sat upon, thirty-two people have squeezed in there to ask questions, or give belligerent arguments. There have been people from the theatre, scientists, engineers, doctors, artists, architects, lawyers, writers, secretaries, nurses, theological students, and many other varieties of students. But the flat was only "one stop" on the English trips, as days were divided among Oxford, Cambridge, Glasgow and St. Andrews as well as London, and intensive evenings were spent in discussion with an amazing collection of people. This in turn brought more people to the chalet, wanting to go on with what had merely had a beginning in a five-hour evening of talking!

Yes . . . Hilary's gift that opened the first English trip was, it would seem, clearly something God "led" her to give, but it involved her willingness to *act* upon that strong inward certainty that she should do it. The results are immeasurable.

The chapel being built

CHAPTER NINETEEN

A Community is born

At times when I wanted to get away to a hidden quiet spot to read or pray alone, I would run across the road, down a bit, up a path that went sharply back to the left, and I'd be in the garden of Chalet le Chesalet. The owners only came for a few weeks during the year, or a week-end now and then, and the view and quietness took one miles away . . . though it was a stone's throw from the front hedge of Les Mélèzes, hidden by a dip in the hill. Chesalet was a barn back in 1711, made of enormous rough hewn heavy wood, now darkened with stain through the years. An artist of an architect and an artist of an interior decorator had combined their imaginations and the poetry of their ideas to make it into a chalet that has everything a chalet should have: inside and out, charming, livable, the sort of place you look at, and sigh deeply about . . . wishing you had time to just sit down and enjoy it! I used to dream about Chesalet being a part of *L'Abri*, but it seemed a daydream indeed.

Then one morning I went down there to find the owner shaking out the feather "puffs" that billow over Swiss beds to keep one as warm as toast. I spoke to her, complimenting her on her perfectionist tastes as seen in the chalet. She offered to show me through it, and the "sigh" became a deeper one! Then she said that several people had wanted to buy it, "But although it *is* for sale, we only want to sell it to the *right* person. . . ." One could see that she had sentiment about this chalet, and was in no hurry to turn it over into the hands of an insensitive person.

It was at that point my hopes leaped . . . and that leap combined itself with a sudden memory of a long-ago conversation. I remembered that Betty had said that she would like to have a chalet in Switzerland some day, near us, where she could write.

"Fran," I said hesitatingly as I got back to our chalet, "I wonder whether Betty might . . ."

And he said, "Why don't you write and tell her about it. She might be coming over again some time soon, and she could come and look at it."

The letter went off before the second English trip, which was to be in August of that same summer. Betty's reply was swift and surprising: "Your letter brought me a streak of bright lightning. 'This is it'. I was certain. I am asking you to buy Le Chesalet for me; please arrange all the details."

As we prayed for the possibility of fitting in such a request before going on the approaching English trip, we found an answer in a perfect "fitting in" of a stop in Basle at the owner's home, on our trip to Zürich for a Bible class which had been started there in Liselotte's home.

The owners of Le Chesalet wanted to know all about our work. The telling of "the story" of the way we were brought to Huémoz seemed to convince them that our friend Betty, who wanted to be near us, would be the "right sort of person" to buy their beloved chalet. The arrangements began to be made, then and there.

Leaving Belfast, Ireland, in a downpour of rain at eight o'clock one morning, we walked up our own steps in the late afternoon sunshine of the same day, to be greeted by Susan's hugs and this greeting: "Welcome back, I've been corresponding with Betty Carlson about the Chesalet business, and I've just sent a telegram . . . hope I did the right thing."

Within a few days the chalet keys were turned over to us, and the chalet belonged to Betty. It was in perfect condition, with fresh sheets on the beds, silver in the drawers, all the dishes needed for ordinary daily needs. Its perfectionist owner had seen that it looked as she would have liked it to look for her own very special guests.

At first Betty wrote and told us just to use it as a place for "extra quiet", and for whatever needs it would fulfil in *L'Abri*. Chesalet became a place for special teas, for quiet conversations, for prayer meetings, for someone needing extra sleep and rest, and a thousand other things. Betty expected to come and write there some day, but the moment had not yet arrived. It met a multitude of needs and caused us to have many times of absolutely spontaneous thankfulness to the One who had known them and planned for us.

It was on April 6th (it is jotted in the margin of my Bible) that I was sitting in the window of Chesalet in a big chair, with my Bible on my lap, open at Psalm 21, and praying, when I looked out over the fields below Chesalet and began to pray very definitely for a chapel which seemed, even at that time, to be a need. As I prayed and then looked out over fields to the mountains and valleys beyond it seemed to me (not in a vision, but in vivid imagination) that I saw Jane's costumes spread out in a rectangle, rising up as though a person were in them, holding hands like paper cut into dolls, and then turning into wood, to form the sides of a simple chalet-chapel building. I reached for my pen and wrote, "Jane's costumes, sell soon, Lord", beside the verses in that psalm: "Thou hast given him his heart's desire, and hast not withholden the request of his lips. . . . Be thou exalted, Lord, in thine own strength: so will we sing and praise thy power."

Was it my idea to sell Jane's precious costumes? Oh no, not at all. But to know why this came into my mind, you need to hear something of what had happened to Jane.

After Jane became a Christian at the chalet that Easter, she had gone on in opera, singing lead parts as she had before. She felt the Lord gave her His help in her singing, and really wanted to use this talent for *His* glory rather than hers. She began to talk to others, inviting them to the Milan class, when they were there. She began reading the Bible through at the rate of three times a year—three times all the way—and added Christian biographies and theological studies as well as devotional studies to her Bible reading. Then she started taking Bible courses by correspondence, working on them even in her dressing room at times. Gradually a struggle began to take place. It was not prompted by anyone's suggestions, but came from within herself. She began to feel a conflict between the parts with which she identified herself in the operas, and the deepening spiritual person she was becoming. She felt that the struggles at times made it almost impossible for her to pray.

Try as she would to push this aside, she realised she must face the question as to who came first, and whether she was being honest in saying, "I want *Thy* will, Lord, whatever it is."

When a life-time of preparation for a career such as opera is behind one, and a love of it is added to that; and when one is close to the very top rung of the "ladder", it is not a simple thing to jump off, give the ladder a kick, and walk down along a dusty road saying honestly, "wherever You lead me, Lord, I'll follow."

Jane gave hints in letters of what was going on within her, and I ached over it with her. There was the time when she wrote of her niece drawing in her breath when she finished listening to Jane tell an exciting Bible story, and exclaiming, "Oh, Aunt Jane, when you are old, and your voice is cracked— you know what you ought to be, you ought to be a missionary."

Jane in the midst of her struggle thought often of those words: "When you are old, and your voice is cracked, then..." And she prayed for a particular sign that the Lord would show her whether the time had come to give up opera while her voice was at its best. That sign was given, and Jane wrote: "Giving up opera, praise God." But the final step became too hard a thing to take, and was put off a bit longer.

On her way by air from Paris to Geneva in January . . . an engine of the plane failed. The passengers were told to remove glasses and so on, and directions were phoned to Geneva airport to prepare the field for a crash landing. Ambulances and fire-fighting equipment were in readiness. Jane prayed. As her whole life suddenly seemed to slide past her eyes like a film, there was nothing that seemed important except doing the Lord's will. What would be worth while if she were ushered immediately into God's presence? "Oh Lord, if it be Thy will, please give me a longer time; please bring this plane in safely, and the rest of my life belongs to You in a very real way."

A silence fell upon the whole planeful of passengers as the plane glided to the ground with scarcely a bad bump . . . and then, a cheer broke out! But no one knew the full extent of all that had been going on in a "battle in the unseen world", invisible to human eyes. Jane telephoned the chalet that midnight hour, and asked if she could come as a Worker at *L'Abri*.

Early in the spring, before that April 6th day of prayer, Jane had thought of her costumes, lying folded away in trunks in a dusty attic in Milan. In that prayertime she gave them to the Lord. Now that was real enough—a relinquishing—but in practical terms, how do you give to the Lord opera costumes designed to fit, not only a person's measurements, but specific parts in specific operas?

The prayer for a buyer for those costumes seemed one of the most impossible requests we had ever made. It was over a year before it was answered.

A telegram one day informed Jane that a singer wanted to look at her costumes. The singer said she was only interested in one or two, and Jane was only interested in selling them as a complete wardrobe. So with very little expectation Jane watched the singer trying them on. One after another they fitted perfectly! Even more amazingly, the discovery was made that this singer sang the same parts as Jane. She needed the costumes for the specific operas for which they had been designed! So Jane's costumes became a part of the "chapel fund".

Now, several times since we had begun praying for a chapel there had seemed to be possibilities of building one, but each time these hopeful possibilities melted away, and we knew that for some reason it was not yet the right time for it.

The day came when Betty felt certain that it was right to come and make her home in her own chalet. She and Jane made Chesalet into another home unit of our unusual little "community". Sunday morning breakfasts for *L'Abri* guests became a part of Chesalet's contribution, as well as the "choir practice" Jane conducted there, giving a musical outlet for nurses and therapists at Bellevue, as well as others.

The garden at Chesalet grew thriving vegetables. Betty and Jane began to talk over gardening problems with their next-door neighbour, whom we always called "the Bee man", because he kept bees, as well as sheep and lambs, and was an expert in the growing of fruit trees, as well as in making cheese. The Bee man was a good person to consult on many questions. As Betty speaks French, and Jane German, and the Bee man both French and German, their conversations together were a bit unusual. As English was not used, Betty and Jane couldn't understand each other, but the Bee man could understand both of them!

In this strange language combination, conversations began to get on to things concerning Christianity, and the Bible, and eventually the three were having Bible studies together. The Bee man's interest grew and grew . . . until the wonderful day when things came into focus for him as he heard the answers being given to his questions. He was one of the most profoundly changed people we have ever seen.

The Bee man had a plot of ground, and a foundation of a chalet started on it. It was situated across a lower dirt road, below the field and below Chesalet. He had intended to build a chalet there to sell. As months went on, and he not only studied his German Bible and pored over his huge Bible dictionary finding things that excited him, but also came to the church services and Sunday evening teas and other community times, the Bee man began to measure the square metres in the Mélèzes living-room, and the possible number of square metres if his foundations were enlarged to build a slightly larger chalet. He then began to tell us of the ideas simmering in his mind, and entering his conscious prayers.

"I would like to turn my chalet plans into a simple chapel building. I could not give my whole time building it, yet I could build it for less than a commercial builder . . . and I would do it with such love, my whole heart would be in it. It would be the joy of my life to build a worship place for this growing little community in which I am finding so much happiness."

There was need to pray for an amount of money that would indicate to us that the Lord was unfolding this as a part of His plan, and that we would not be rushing into something of our own planning. The human tendency is to feel that "now the time has come to act" and to be too impatient to "wait". That feeling was a danger in this situation, after waiting so long for the chapel to become a reality. But we did go slowly, and we felt God gave us His leading.

The end of this portion of the story cannot be told. At this present time of writing, the framework of the chapel is going up higher every day, and the roof will soon be on so that the men can continue to work throughout the winter, without worrying about the weather. It almost seems like a mirage, as we wind up the road on the yellow bus and see that new building in plain sight so much of the way, and know that it is a chapel for *L'Abri*. What is going to take place in it? Who will come to services from the ski centres so close to us when there is a building to come to rather than a living-room of a private home, which no one knows houses a Sunday service? We have no idea . . . and we ourselves are waiting with interest to read that next chapter when it begins to be written in the life of our community.

Community? What community?

We started, as you know, by coming to Chalet les Mélèzes—without knowing what we were really going to be doing there at all. Half of Chalet Beau Site was the first addition, and then Chesalet. The rehabilitation home for cerebral palsy children, and all the staff over there, were "community" with us, without being a part of *L'Abri* at all. They are a separate medical work, recognised by the Swiss medical society. Chesalet is Betty's home, and Betty is an independent journalist and writer of books, not a *L'Abri* Worker. She is just living there because she has chosen to come into this "community". Next door to Chesalet is the Bee man's chalet, which has two apartments. He lives in the upper one.

Downstairs live Mr. and Mrs. Martin. After Linette had been a Worker for over two years—she was a student in the University of Lausanne, bringing up other students for weekends—she felt that God had definitely guided her to visit members of the Praying Family in America. (These are people who pledged to the Lord to pray for *L'Abri* for definite periods of time each day. They have not been asked to do this, but have themselves written asking to be a part of the work through specific prayer.) Linette was curious to meet these people, and to give them a more personal view of *L'Abri*, rather than just written accounts. Before she left, she realised that she was in love with one, Joe Martin, a Harvard graduate, with two years of postgraduate study at Princeton, who had been a *L'Abri* Worker for some time. Six months later Joe went to America, and while Linette was a guest in his parents' home they became engaged. After their marriage they lived in the Bee man's downstairs apartment, as *L'Abri* Workers.

The entire house of Beau Site is now in use, with Ranald Macaulay of Cambridge University, and his wife—our Susan—and their little Margaret as the ones in charge.

When Priscilla and John had been in America for four years, and John had completed his theological studies, they felt certain that God was leading them into *L'Abri* work, at least for a time. The first winter of their return they shared Beau Site with Susan and Ranald and the others who lived there. Then, just before little Rebecca was born (their second girl)—in June 1963—they had an "impossible" answer to prayer. After a fruitless search for a chalet for months, suddenly a woman decided to let hers, which she had kept as a summer home, for the first time. Now Priscilla, John and the two very little girls live in Chalet Tzi No, and have room for six guests, as well as taking their turn in having people for meals and "conversations".

There have been various people who have come to live near *L'Abri* for shorter or longer periods of time. One family came for six months, as the father studied at Farel House, and the family took part in the "community life". This family lived in the village in a rented chalet. As I write, two families are doing that, living opposite each other, right in the centre of the village. In one lives a widowed mother and her four children. Mrs. Kramer is a violinist. She felt a strong certainty that she should come for a year, to be near *L'Abri*, as well as to study the violin under a "master" who is living in Switzerland at present.

The other family consists of Swiss Claudie—the one who came from Montreux. Her husband, Allan, left his pastorate in the States, and came over to be near *L'Abri*, and study in Farel House. He is a graduate of a very "liberal" theological school which would be horrified at our "conservative" beliefs. Two tiny boys are part of Claudie and Allan's contribution to the community Sunday school. Allan teaches in a nearby boarding school to make it possible for them to be here at all.

A car from Lausanne brings Harro and Ann to *L'Abri* frequently enough to be included in this description of the community. Dutch Harro was a strong, argumentative atheist when he first came to the chalet back in 1960 for weekends. It seemed impossible that he could be one who would ever be affected by the message of the Bible. But not only did he become a Christian, he also married Ann, an English-Swiss girl brought up in Egypt, who also became a believer at the chalet. When he graduated from the university, and married Ann, he took a job in Lausanne and settled there. They belong to our little International Church, and they have a Bible class in their apartment in Lausanne, which Fran leads every other Wednesday evening. They come as frequently as possible to the chalet for weekends, though baby Tessa makes that harder since she joined the family.

The International Church may sound like a big name for a little group of believers. It simply indicates that the membership is made up of people from a variety of countries. Members are those who live in our community, or who have desired to have their membership with this group where they feel they have their spiritual home. There is no pressure to make this little church larger by adding members. It is in existence because of a need, not because we want to begin to pile up statistics. Most people who come to *L'Abri* don't even know of its existence. Facts about its existence and origin are not even spoken of in the services on Sunday, as they are for worship and the study of the Bible.

But to have a full picture of the community that has grown as a plant putting out new shoots, you need to know about the International Church. The Sunday school has several little classes meeting at different times of the day. There is one for the tiny toddlers which one mother teaches while the others go to church. There is one for the older children in the afternoon. There are several at the cerebral palsy home, in German and in French for different age groups. And there is the "hymn sing" on Sundays led by Jane, also over at the rehabilitation home, so that the children can have the joy of music, and keep time with their movements, even if they cannot sing. The accompaniment is Mary's harpsichord, and some flutes, recorders, a violin and a cello. It is quite an experience to take part in it.

I often remember that first Easter Sunday at Mélèzes, sitting at a table by the hedge in the utter quietness of a place where we had no one to talk to about Christian things, looking over in the direction of the curve of the mountain that hid Champéry and wondering—wondering why we had been torn away from what seemed a growing, fruitful work. "What are we going to do here?" was the deep question inside; a question we hardly dared voice, except to God in prayer.

As I look around at all the people gathered at a high tea on a Sunday—often as many as fifty—and look from face to face thinking of how many of them became Christians at *L'Abri*; remember how many atheists are now Christians; become bewildered at trying to sort out the happenings of the succession of years, or trying to remember the varieties of people, let alone all the individuals, who have come, and been affected in their coming: as I look around I feel a little shudder of another kind.

What if . . . we had decided to plan the work ourselves? What if . . . we had not thrown ourselves upon the reality of prayer, and God's promises to answer . . . and His ability to carry out His promises of guiding His children? What would have been missed?

Statue of William Farel, Neuchâtel

CHAPTER TWENTY

"It's worth it all"

THE CHICKENS were in the oven roasting with a square of oiled cloth over them to keep them moist, the table was set and the pine cone and blue spruce centrepiece looked satisfyingly lovely with the dull green candles in the low silver holders, and a few silver Christmas tree balls gleaming with just the right bit of brightness among the woodsy browns and greens. "There. Now I'll hurry and finish dressing for church, there isn't much time left. Are the chairs all down there? Has someone put on music?" It was January 3rd, and the chalet was full of people who had come for "over New Year's".

"Mother!"

I opened the office door pulling my dress over my head, and noticed that Susan was carrying a big white sheet of paper with something written on it: "Mother". Her tone of voice and that paper, gave me a sudden feeling of dread to hear the sentence that was coming.

"Susan, is it bad news?"

"Yes, Mother, I'm afraid it is."

"Susan . . . is it my mother?"

"Yes."

I read the paper, with its message that had been phoned from the telegraph office in Lausanne and written down in Liselotte's handwriting: "Wilmington—2nd—9.17 p.m.—Mother fell asleep in Jesus about six—funeral Dr. Laird—love—Father."

The tears flowed suddenly, and my first cry was, "Oh, but I wanted to tell her about . . . I wanted to write her tomorrow and . . ."

There it was, the wall of separation that death puts up against communication! That *enemy* death. I remembered her face as she waved at the dock in New York. I hadn't seen her since. It had been six years. But we had had communication, plenty of it, and had been close in our thinking.

It's the separation that is so hard—the separation of friend from friend in such a "total" way, no way to get through, separation of body from soul. Suddenly the personality has gone. It's this that the Bible is talking about when it says that Jesus came to have victory over death, the horrible enemy which was a result of sin. The exchange is terrific . . . Christ died—to give life. Eternal life in the words of the Bible means life in a resurrected body.

How can there be a resurrection? How could Jesus rise again? Those who saw Him alive didn't believe their eyes at first. "How can it be?" is the question of every human being when faced with things he doesn't understand.

What difficulty would it be for God, if there is a God, to raise from the dead that which He designed and put together in the first place? And how could He tell us more clearly than He already has, first by example—showing us the resurrection through Christ's dying and then rising on the third day, eating, talking, moving among people for forty days—and then by written words, telling us that Christ was, after the resurrection, able to do the same things He was able to do in His body?

I believe it to be true. I know I shall see Mother, and other people I'm waiting to see, in the body, with an eternity of time to spend communicating! This is the "glorious hope" we have, as we wait for that day to come.

Why then did I weep? Do we not weep when someone goes thousands of miles away, and the day-by-day talk over a cup of tea is cut off? We are not wood and stone, and our emotions are real. But we weep not as ones who have no hope, no assurance of the future.

Dear Mother had folded 1,300 "Family Letters", the mimeo-graphed story-account I had written in November, and she had added a personal note to them. She had "stuffed the envelopes" on New Year's day, then the next day she was "absent from the body, and present with the Lord", with no warning.

That took place just before Jane Stuart Smith's arrival. Then, in the spring, Jane was there to help the handful of young people who were going to go right on with *L'Abri* through the spring, without Fran, myself, Franky or Debby. A round-trip freighter ticket for the four of us was practically given to us by a Christian man whose business included ship-ping, and we were on our way to see my father, who now was alone, and to spend some time with Fran's mother. None of us knew that God was taking us at that time because Franky needed a muscle transplant operation to give more normal movement in his foot and leg. We discovered that later. None of us knew that Jane's help would be suddenly interrupted by a telephone call to inform her of her mother's immediate need of her because of the sudden death of her beloved father.

When we left we expected to be back on the freighter's second trip back. We left Jane in Chesalet. Ranald (who had finished his studies in law at Cambridge and had entered theological school, but felt he would learn more at *L'Abri*) had come at the end of March as a Worker and was taking care of Beau Site. Trudy and Linette were caring for Mélèzes. Boys would be put in Beau Site, and girls in the other two chalets when weekend guests, or others arrived. We felt it would be for a short few weeks.

That summer had a purpose in it. It was a summer that taught us all new reality in trusting God's leading, in praying with faith believing that God could do all things.

For instance, it had become pretty normal to expect to see Fran in the red barrel chair on Saturday nights, and to expect him to answer the questions in a way that would take the wind out of the "stock questions" and cause some thinking. It had become pretty normal to expect gardens and meals to be planned and cared for in my department. Everyone helped, but days of prayer, spontaneous conversations in the kitchen, the routine things and special decisions fell into the responsibility in a natural way of two people; and the feeling that the personality of these two people had a lot to do with results crept into attitudes. . . .

That summer gave us new lessons in the fact that God really was the One who was planning.

Soon after we left, Linette wrote a breathless letter about Ina's first weekend there—Ina, who now is Fritz's wife.

"Ina walked up to the front door the next morning, vivacious, dark-haired, in a pink cotton dress . . . and we found out that she was a refugee from Eastern Germany. That evening we sat around the living-room and talked among ourselves of our joy in the Lord. Then Ranald turned to Ina, sitting very quietly, and said, 'Do you have any questions or anything you would like to talk about?'

"Wistfully Ina said, 'I've never heard anything like this before. I was confirmed in a Lutheran Church, but *this* is all so new!' How familiar that sounded to us: 'But it was just the same with me . . .' 'I went to church for years and never knew . . .' And then Ranald began at the very beginning, while Ina listened intently."

Linette went on to tell of the excitement that ran through the household when the news was told that Ina had become a Christian. They couldn't believe it, that it had happened like this, just themselves, alone.

Who were the "Workers"?

There was Linette, young and fresh out of ballet; Trudy, young and a Swiss secretary; Ranald, young and a law graduate; Jane, newly having left her successful opera career. There was no one with years of "theological training". I'm not belittling study and knowledge and preparation, I'm just trying to tell you what was shown of "reality". Teenaged Barney, my nephew, was a part of the household, and Olave, a South African girl, came up weekends, bringing university students with her. . . .

Then, in June, Jane was called suddenly away on a Sunday morning, and Franky had his operation, delaying us until September (which in itself was another whole story of answered prayer and God's guidance), and the handful left there looked at each other in dismay.

"The whole long summer ahead of us. *L'Abri*'s busiest time. Gardens. People to talk to. Meals. How *can* we?". . . .

Susan was at Dorset House School of Occupational Therapy in Oxford at that time, with no real summer vacation period ahead of her. When she found out the plight of the Workers at the chalet, she prayed for guidance as to her responsibility, then went to see her principal. The result? An unprecedented exception was made, and Susan was allowed to study anatomy and psychology at home while she pitched in and worked like mad, cooking, gardening and talking to people. She went back in November and took her exams, passing them with honours; in fact, she was third from the top in all of England in that set of exams. She felt she had been clearly led by the God whom she knew as her Father, to put Him first and go back to help, praying for His help in her studying under such difficult conditions. The results, she felt, showed that she had not misunderstood. This was without our knowledge even, until the decision had been made; we had put no human pressure on either side.

Their summer was an extremely hard one. Two college girls, Patsy and Elizabeth, from homes of a measure of luxury, came to help. They were immersed in mountains of potato and apple peels, and were amazed at the frugal use of boiled chicken bones for delicious broth, and the using up of every scrap of edible food—even the making of jelly from the apple peelings left after pies had been put into the oven.

It was a summer of hard work for the bunch of young people who were there, but the spiritual results said something to us all. Ina was not the only one. Jim and Morris were results of that summer—teenage sons of a brilliant atheist, they had been brought up to have no religion. Both of them became Christians, and one is in a California university today, the other in Harvard, neither one swerving in his beliefs. Udo came for the first time that summer. A German law student, Udo was an agnostic who had no idea of doing anything except showing the logic of his position. The first weekend we arrived back from America blond, smiling Udo was introduced to us as a Christian who had been "born" into the family, with Ranald's help. Lindsay, an Oxford agnostic, was also one who came to a decision that the Bible is truth during that summer. These weren't "Kentucky mountain children", but strong-minded, educated, intellectual young people.

That summer we had a demonstration of reality that we can't take for granted and will never forget.

Then a new step was shown us, a new "thread" was introduced into the weaving, a new page was turned by God. How does it work? This being led by God in a work together, not just in an individual life? Perhaps this will illustrate it as well as anything so far.

There was no herald of trumpets, no impressive noises, smells, sights, or feeling. There was just a letter, or rather two letters, delivered on Long Island where we were staying as Franky recuperated from his operation. One came from Ranald, saying he felt that he would like to take an external degree from the University of London, meaning that he could stay on and help in the work, yet study half days towards a theological degree. Work on this could be done anywhere; examinations are taken in a British Embassy at the appointed time.

Another letter came at the same time from Deirdre and Richard. Deirdre had given up her art job, Richard his pilot's job and they were headed for a school in California where Richard would enter an engineering course.

"May we come and study at *L'Abri* first for six months? We feel it is the preparation we need."

Three people wanted to study at *L'Abri*. But where?

"Well, there is the sunroom at Beau Site."

They wanted to help with the work, listen in to conversations, and study. We thought of the needed equipment: desks, books.

And then we remembered.

"Farel was forced out of Huémoz during the time of the Reformation in that part of Switzerland. Farel believed the same truth we believe, and risked his life to preach it boldly. Let's call our study place 'Farel House', remembering him."

What a perfect name to say what we wanted it to say, and

to fit in with the village where God put us. Farel, running down the hill centuries ago, alive, a man with earnest beliefs but as real a personality as one could be—chased by village women with their laundry sticks, throwing things at the young Reformer! What a fitting name for this modest new enterprise, both for the sunroom, and the young "Farels" who were to study there.

The Evangelical Library in London wrote to Jane Stuart Smith at just that time, because she had been borrowing books by mail at a staggering rate. The letter asked whether she knew if we might be interested in a branch library at *L'Abri*.

A library? Farel House needed a library. And so packages of books began arriving, open at one end in the regulation manner. These theological books were brought up by Alice in the little wagon from the post office, opened by Jane, listed and catalogued.

Mr. Dubi made measurements for desks—five at first, then two more—with room to spread out reference books, a shelf for individual study books and ink, pens, and shelves in the bedroom adjoining the sunroom which, devoid of beds, became the branch of the Evangelical Library!

So Farel House started. Guidance? We hadn't planned it, or worked towards such a thing. But it was, we feel, God's plan for that time, and for however long He wants to use it to meet a need.

Then, in mid-December, two depressing pieces of news came to our attention. One was that the funds were so low it seemed that for the first time in *L'Abri*, the end of the year, December 31st, would come with not enough to pay the bills. The second was that Beau Site's two owner brothers had decided to sell Beau Site. Not enough money for the month, at the year's end—and a house we needed more than ever, because of Farel House, to be sold from under us!

Franky was having his bath when he called out, "Debby, Susan, come and have prayer. Mommy and Daddy are talking to the Anex man from Zürich, and we don't have any money to buy Beau Site." Cosily dried and in his bathrobe, it was Franky at that time who led the girls, Linette joining them, in praying for the Lord's solution to this terrific problem.

Far off in Nova Scotia lives an elderly lady who is shut away because of deafness from much she could enjoy of the voices and music of this world. But she is a person who is particularly acute in her "spiritual hearing"; someone who is close to the God who is her Father. One night she was lying awake, unable to sleep, thinking about *L'Abri*, for which she prays daily. She began to pray, very specifically: "Oh Lord, cause the two brothers who own Beau Site to rent it at a very cheap price for many years, and give *L'Abri* enough money to do the needed repairs on the place so that it will be suitable for Farel House."

She had written to me of that prayer, and of her strong conviction that God had led her in it, that this was going to be the solution. Frankly I smiled with a feeling of warm pleasure at her naïvety. "That", I thought, "that is about the most impossible thing I've ever heard. These men will never change their minds, they want to get rid of the place. Anyway, Fran will never put money in a rented house again, not after Champéry. So it isn't possible. Dear Mrs. MacMullen. . . ."

Down in the living-room by the fireplace three people sat, each a bit nervous as to the outcome of the time together. I began in French to explain that we did not have the money to buy, and suddenly I found myself launching forth into the story of *L'Abri*, of answered prayer, and of how Farel House had started. I condensed quite a bit. It was all in my faulty French, but the bank clerk got misty-eyed, and he said, "I'd like our old home to be used for a study place like that . . . named after Farel. Let's meet again in a couple of months, and wait to see if the money comes to you while you pray for it." Even that much seemed an amazing answer to prayer right then.

Christmas came with no answer as to our needed money. It seemed a heaviness was in the air. We wondered whether we should even have a big Christmas dinner. Then on Christmas Eve the phone rang, and a "once-in-history" invitation was given. Monsieur T. who had come to our church service occasionally was saying that he had a small heart attack, so that he would not be allowed out of the house for a Christmas service.

"I have a very selfish request," he said. "Would *L'Abri* come to me for dinner, and would Mr. Schaeffer preach, in my living-room, a Christmas sermon for us all?"

Taxis came for us all—fifteen of us—and we not only had a Christmas dinner—"with no dishes to do"—but this family had saved their tree to enjoy with us. In Switzerland people "have a tree", which means a moment comes when all the candles are lighted, sparklers are set off (sending showers of starry sprays for a few moments of sheer glory)—and the tree has been "had".

Gifts were given out to their children, Franky and Debby included, and the man came over and placed an envelope "for *L'Abri*" in my lap. One peek at the cheque clipped to the Christmas card caused me to gasp. The Lord had chosen this unique way to answer our total need for the month, and the year was going to close with all expenses met once again!

When it was time to meet the owner in Zürich to talk about Beau Site, two things had become clear. We were not going to be able to buy the house, but God had sent in an amount which would cover needed repairs, including a badly needed second bathroom. One of these gifts had staggered us all. It had been the entire bank account of a nurse in America, who wrote that while she was praying one morning she felt she could not say honestly, "I trust you with my whole life, God", without showing it to God by giving away her bank account. She had gone to the bank on her way to the hospital and drawn out 1,000 dollars, leaving the account empty, and sent it "For Beau Site"—for she had visited *L'Abri* when Beau Site had become a problem.

The owners had come to their decision, and that day we were told: "We will rent the whole house for the price we used to rent half . . . and we will give you a twelve-year contract at that price. You will agree to do the repairs." There were exceptions that they were going to take care of, such as the roof and so on.

So Farel House had a place in which to continue.

In the next April there was another wedding, and Susan and Ranald became Mr. and Mrs. Macaulay, in the same Ollon church. They left for a honeymoon in South Africa and Rhodesia—a gift of his parents—to visit Ranald's grandmother, aunts and uncles as well as his mother and father, and to introduce Susan to them. When they returned in July, they became the host and hostess of Beau Site, and a new phase of *L'Abri* commenced.

The second year of Farel House there were a few others who wanted a study in *L'Abri*—not as in a school, but doing individual work in a research manner, having discussions and seminars together, and meeting with Fran as Senior Tutor to hear lectures on such subjects as "The Intellectual Climate", "The New Theology", or whatever subject he thought would be helpful to those studying at Farel House at that time.

During the summer of 1962 there were fourteen who came as Farel House students. The next winter a married man came with his family for six months, living in the village; and others came for shorter periods of time. It is not a school in the usual sense of the term, but it is a place where people may come to have a time to study, yet take part in the reality of what is going on in *L'Abri* (including the hard physical work) and to listen to the discussions, learning as people ask actual questions, rather than academically. Farel House is very, very limited in space. But it has had an impact on some lives and in some countries already. We have no knowledge of what God wants to do with it in the future.

We now have several households, as I have outlined to you. People who come are "divided up" for meals. It is a bit complicated for housekeeping and keeping accounts, but it means smaller numbers around a table, gives opportunity for continuing the informal family atmosphere, and encourages conversation around the tables. Everyone sacrifices "family life" to include a larger number in the families. Obviously this creates problems in our own family life. There is no "pat solution" to this. We do, however, go through struggles, and need to keep praying for God's solutions rather than our own sudden clever ideas for working things out.

Not everyone who has come to *L'Abri* has gone away believing, by any means. I must make that clear. Nor has everyone who has believed continued to live a Christian life. Nor has everyone who has continued to live a Christian life changed his or her profession. The instances given have been chosen with a desire to show what we believe God has done. There is much more that could be told, on the positive side, and there are many people who could be mentioned who came to *L'Abri* but in whose lives we have no knowledge of a lasting effect.

A family comes to Switzerland: a family, cast out, ends up on the side of a mountain, half-way up to a ski resort, in a place whose name is not even well known.

The story has been a story of the reality of what God has done. But the story has not ended. It is in the middle of "being done" now, what God brought us all here to do.

What about the future? Not one of us would know any more than we did in the beginning. But we know this. *L'Abri* is God's plan, of that we are convinced. He will continue it in the form in which He has planned it, if we do not hinder Him by letting self-will get in the way.

Each one of us as an individual would feel himself to be in direct contact with God. We know that as long as we are together here there is a blended work to be done. But any one of us could be led *out* into some other plan God may have for us; out of this location, or out of *L'Abri* into something else. We are individuals before God, and we believe He can deal with us as individuals. We have no binding human contract for life. Our binding contract is with God. As a work, as a group, we pray unitedly for agreement and accord among us in decisions to be made. We pray that His guidance may be clear to us as a group, for we feel the blending of so many personalities is as important as a demonstration of reality as the individual guidance is.

Will it work? The story has already covered a period of eight years. We are ordinary, imperfect, sinful people. There is nothing special about us. This is not a Utopia, in any sense. But in the small measure in which we have come to put self aside, and to wait for God's direction, we have found, and will find, reality in a two-way communication with God.

There are, and always will be, many places for improvement in our struggle to be honest before God, hour by hour, day by day, month by month. So there are, and will be many places for improvement in that which is to be seen by other eyes.

This is not a life of ease, but a life of tremendous excitement, in between the struggles: excitement because of finding that we are in contact with the supernatural today.

The chapel, L'Abri

SUNDAY AUGUST 11, 1968

LES MELEZES HELPERS

MENUS ❋

SUNDAY LUNCH

EGG STRING SOUP

SPECIAL CHINESE MEAL
with CHICKEN and PORK
GARDEN VEGETABLES
and ALMONDS

VANILLA ICE CREAM
with Chocolate Sauce

Coffee — Tea

FAVORITE ICE CREAM RECIPE (COPY IF YOU WANT IT TO TAKE HOME)
2 CUPS of Whipping Cream.
2 CUPS of Milk (or 3 regular Cream
1½ Cups of Sugar 1 milk)
STIR UNTIL SUGAR DISOLVES
FREEZE — Whip after frozen firm
until very fluffy + smooth it
increases in bulk — Whip with
ELECTRIC BEATER — do not underbeat!
Refreeze

CHOCOLATE SAUCE
3 CUPS SUGAR — ½ CUP COCOA
1 CUP MILK — STIR WELL
BOIL 4 MIN. add ¼ C. butter
BOIL 4 MIN. again — then beat until looses gloss
CUT IN DAINTY SHAPES.

HIGH TEA

Egg — CUCUMBER with Parsley
TUNA with Celery
Snipped mint + lemon
Peanut Butter + honey
Tomato + lettuce
Cream Cheese + Ginger
TOASTED CHEESE
SANDWICHES
Rolled —
4 fingers to each SLICE

Homemade Orange Rolls
Homemade Raisin Bread
SPREAD BREAD OUT TO THE EDGES!

WORK ❋

PREPARE AS MUCH AS
POSSIBLE on SATURDAY
MAKE MAYONAISE FIRST
CHINESE DINNER
RECIPE

CUT ONIONS IN RINGS:
← Like This
CUT CELERY "ROOT" AND
BRANCH CELERY
BRANCH ROOT

PICK + WASH CHINESE
CABBAGE CUT IN SHREDS

PICK ZUCHINNI SQUASH
CUT IN RINGS
DO NOT PEEL CUT ⅛" thick

OPEN 1 CAN (TIN for you English)
OF PINEAPPLE —
CUT IN SMALL WEDGES

ROAST CHICKEN + PORK
IN LOW OVEN (200°)
until Partially cooked
HAVE ALL READY FOR LAST
MINUTE ASSEMBLING —
CUT CHICKEN + PORK
IN finger STRIPS —

HEAT OIL IN Large pot.
Put in meat strips —
Then onions and celery
THEN WATER ⅔ of the final amount
Add Knorr Chicken Boullion
Accent and Soya Sauce
THICKEN with CORN STARCH
and cold water —
When Boiling add other
things .... cook 3 MIN.
SERVE ON RICE — TOP
with Blanched Toasted
Almonds —

CHAPTER TWENTY-ONE

And Five Years later

RIP VAN WINKLE had a perspective sharpened by a gap of twenty years' sleep! It was an advantage, as he could suddenly see the changes and results of history without having lived through it. In the first twenty chapters you have lived through about fifteen years of our lives. Now in this last chapter you will have a Rip Van Winkle perspective of *L'Abri* today, as five years have gone by between writing chapter twenty and chapter twenty-one.

Remember the promise I felt God had given us, way back in an early chapter of the book? That verse from Isaiah 2:2. This past Saturday night, in mid-July 1968, Fran and I stood looking over the balcony at the people below on the terrace. We couldn't help thinking out loud of that verse: "And all nations shall flow unto it. And many people shall go and say, Come ye, and let us go up to the mountain of the Lord . . . and he will teach us of his ways . . ."

"Fran, that's what one hundred and twenty-five people look like. Come on up to the end of the balcony and look over. They're scattered on that side too."

Fran had been sitting at the foot of our bed (his desk still, as he sits on a rocking chair working on the end of the bed), preparing his sermon for the wedding to be held in the middle of the service the next day. My apron was stained and my hands still crumby from making (along with Cynthia and several helpers) the food to fill those 125 plates . . . but we had come out for a minute to look down in utter wonder at the people below.

Who are they? Professors, pastors, doctors, lawyers, artists, architects, writers, musicians, nurses, schoolteachers, secretaries, scientists, actors, and students of all kinds and varieties—as well as drop-outs and opt-outs! There were Japanese studying in Germany, French, Italians, Germans, Dutch, English, Scots, Irish, Canadians, Americans from many different states, Swiss, South Americans, Scandinavians, Australians, New Zealanders and South Africans. There were long-haired boys, and a wide variety of beards and dress; long-haired girls, the beatniky types and the ultra-fashionable types; the ones who had just arrived for the first time, and the *L'Abri* Family ones who had become Christians and had come back bringing friends. There were Christian workers, pastors and professors seeking help in understanding the twentieth-century young people—and "less respectable" young people who had already a long history of drug-taking in their search for some sort of meaning to this "meaningless life". Every sort of religious and philosophic background seemed to be represented with a twentieth-century unification among them, in an inability to believe that truth exists—yet with a hunger to find meaning, not being satisfied with the "plastic universe" of today.

We felt emotional as we watched them that Saturday night, because we could trace the history of some of them. Bill, for instance, heard about *L'Abri* as he talked to a girl in Palestine and came to find out for himself, pack on back! Bill, with his handle-bar moustache and his round thin-rimmed "far-out" glasses, had tried everything, including drugs, and had dropped out of an American university, after having had the best of prep. schools and all that a fine established eastern United States family could offer him, to wander in rebellion and search. Bill was now a convinced "child of Abraham" (as he likes to term it) and of Abraham's Messiah. There he was, below, talking earnestly and in great detail to his two friends who had come to study in Farel House too, in their search to see what it was Bill had found so convincing. Then there was

Ian, with his shoulder-length hair and his favourite bright blue felt hat flopping around as he emphasised a point. He too was now talking from the viewpoint of the truth of Christianity, as he became certain of the truth just a couple of weeks before.

Saturday night that week was different in that there was a concert instead of the usual Saturday night discussion led by Fran. The concert was breathtakingly beautiful. Rex thrilled us with Liszt, Jane sang her first operatic aria for eight years, and a Belgian girl skilfully played her violin. Sunday's service was also different, as a wedding was included in the morning service.

Let me tell you this one story briefly. Jack arrived not knowing what *L'Abri* was, right in the middle of Barry and Veronica Seagren's wedding in December. Jack, a Canadian medical student who was going around the world looking for "answers" to life, had come to the right place, he felt, even though he had not known what *L'Abri* was before he came. He had been given our address as the place to meet an old friend. Jack became a Christian so quickly that it took our breath away. (Who can explain why some people understand both intellectually and spiritually so rapidly, when others take so long?) He stayed on to be a Farel House student, listening to tapes at double speed, working early mornings and late nights. Then Jack became a helper and later a Worker, in charge of the carpentry shop of *L'Abri*. Slim, dark, curly-haired, bearded, Jack does everything with rapid decision! He felt certain that God was calling him into further theological study; hence he registered in a seminary in the States. He also felt certain that Christel (a German girl who had come to *L'Abri* as a helper) was the right one for his wife! Now, this Sunday, six months after his arrival, Jack and Christel were married in the middle of the Sunday church service, and left after the reception in mid-afternoon. Jack came in the middle of the first wedding he had ever attended and then left right after his own wedding. Quite a record!

It meant that this weekend included not only serving 125 for Saturday night supper, but decorating a chapel for the wedding (with fern, moss, logs, bricks standing on end, and long-stemmed cultivated daisies) after the concert, then cooking for Sunday after that. Then the morning church service, with the ceremony taking place just before the sermon on marriage, and Sunday dinner—divided among the chalets. Les Mélèzes fed 52 for Sunday dinner, 135 for a wedding reception immediately after, and then 125 for Sunday high tea at seven in the evening. Each of the other chalets had their share of as many people as they could manage, to feed and to find space to sleep. There are double-decker beds, camp beds placed on available floor space, including balconies and living-room floors. It is just as difficult as it was in the beginning, when we had to place mattresses on the floor of Les Mélèzes for the girls coming from Basle. It is simply that there are more chalets and Workers, more people involved in the sacrifice of living this way by faith, and more people involved in coming here to ask questions and study truth.

Let me rapidly outline some of the changes and additions as God has unfolded His plan through these past five years.

Susan and Ranald were caring for Beau Site five years ago; Now they have been the *L'Abri* Workers in England for four years. A very long chapter could be told about the way God provided for a house in Ealing, London, to take the place of the flat in Chelsea. The answers to prayer and the certainty of God's having chosen the house at 52 Cleveland Road, were just as amazing as those connected with the provision of Chalet les Mélèzes. The variety of things which showed that Susan and Ranald should go to England rather than stay in Switzerland were also definite. Ranald has been able to complete an Honours degree in Theology at King's College, London, as well as carry on the *L'Abri* work. Recently the work has grown within that house itself, with Sunday school classes for children, Bible classes, and church services added to discussions, tape-listening sessions, and so on; and floods of invitations are coming to Ranald, as well as to Fran, to speak in various places in England.

Another chapter could be written about the Ashburnham Conference in Sussex; the first complete *L'Abri* conference, this spring, with Fran, Hans Rookmaaker (Professor of Art History at the Free University of Amsterdam), Ranald Macaulay, John Sandri and Hurvey Woodson all lecturing on a wide variety of subjects, with two formal concerts each week by the *L'Abri* Ensemble (Jane Stuart Smith, soprano, Frances Kramer, violin, and Rex Humrich, piano) and an impromptu afternoon concert given by talented guests at the conference. There was a summer Bible school led by Susan for children who came with their parents, giving a very "rounded out" programme, along with talks on prayer and marriage. Norma, who is secretary in Huémoz *L'Abri*, came to help in the registration of guests, assigning people to their rooms and so on, and Sylvia, just arrived from America, released parents to attend the lectures by baby-sitting each evening.

This conference was to meet a need for a place where people in England could come together to hear what they had been asking *L'Abri* speakers to bring to them in a variety of places. Mimeographed notices were sent to the people who seemed interested and even some of those names were left out (as Susan had been the only "office staff" and she had two children and a house to care for as well as other *L'Abri* work). There was none of the usual advertising at all; no notices read out in churches or put in papers or magazines. Yet over 450 people attended for one of the two weeks or for a weekend. The conference buildings did not have space for that many at once, and therefore people were limited in the amount of time they could stay. The variety of people represented a cross-section of the twentieth century once again—as far as age, education, family background, nationality and race were concerned. The Ashburnham Conference was a "first". Is it a pattern for the future? Is it a way for *L'Abri*'s variety of lectures and discussions to be taken to other places? We don't know. All we do know is that we are sure it was the right thing this spring, and it would seem likely to be followed by another in Britain.

What happened to Beau Site as Ranald and Susan left? I mentioned Claudie and Allan earlier in the book. After being Farel House students for a year they asked to stay on as Workers. For two years Allan and Claudie were the Workers caring for Beau Site, and then they felt it right to go to a church in a university town and to use what they had learned at *L'Abri* to help students in America. At that time Nick and Minna were at *L'Abri*. Minna became a Christian at *L'Abri* when she was a sixteen-year-old student at a boarding school in Geneva. She came back when she had completed her university studies and then she became a part of another "*L'Abri* couple" and they took over Beau Site for two years. Now Nick feels it is time to complete his theological course this autumn, along with Jack and Christel, Jerram and Vicki, Pierre and Danielle (the French Jewish Farel House student of the early days) and Barry and Veronica (the ones married the day Jack came). There are also other *L'Abri* Farel House students entering the same theological college: Jim (at present the gardener as a *L'Abri* Worker), Egon (Udo's younger brother who became a Christian through Udo, and has now finished his first university exams in Germany) and Thena, a Canadian girl who came to Farel House rather than take the scholarship offered at Princeton Seminary. That seminary in St. Louis will be flooded with *L'Abri* people this autumn!

St. Louis isn't the only theological school with people "born again" at *L'Abri*, or helped at *L'Abri*, in it. There are three Harvard graduates in a Philadelphia theological school, all three from *L'Abri*, as well as Wellesley girls who have gone there after having been at *L'Abri*, taking classmates with them who through them have become interested in Christianity. There are theological schools in England where people who have been converted at *L'Abri* are preparing for their future work. There are Christian missions and organisations in a number of countries which have people now strong in their work who were not Christians before they came to *L'Abri*. In addition to this there are hundreds of people (or probably thousands, by this time) who have been to *L'Abri* and have seen something which has changed their lives. This "something" is more even than the truth of Christianity. They have come to understand the twentieth-century climate. They have come to realise that there is a possibility of seeing relationships in philosophy, art, history, music, literature, plays and television programmes which opens up to them an understanding of what "is" as well as what is being given, and they have come to a new determination to "think", and then to be creative.

At present Larry and Nancy are the Beau Site couple. Larry came to *L'Abri* about five years ago, having heard about it in a youth hostel in Norway from a fellow who had been here only two days and whose description brings no name to our memories! Larry was another one seeking an answer to life, spending a year in Europe as a possible means of finding that answer, working, travelling and staying in youth hostels. His subject in university was political science. He stayed a year, went back to the States to theological college and came back as a *L'Abri* Worker with his wife Nancy, for a year before finishing his degree. So again Beau Site is cared for.

I mentioned praying for a chalet years ago, and not receiving the money to buy it, but being given the library from it. Chalet les Sapins was the name of that chalet. It was bought by a woman having a vegetarian *pension* connected with a Hindu-type cult. Even when this woman died the probability of the inheritors voting to give the opportunity of buying it to two other parties seemed definite. A woman who had given a whole section of her life to reach people caught up in Hinduism had for a long time wanted to buy it for *L'Abri*'s use, and now perhaps God would use her gift to release a house used for this "ism", although originally built and used by Christians. Perhaps her gift would give the house back to its original use of being a place where the truth of the Bible would be taught. Although it seemed impossible, for legal and currency reasons, it happened. On 20th May, 1967, word came over the telephone to us in Wales, to the buyer in another part of the world, and to *L'Abri* guests by way of ringing cowbells in delightful excitement, that the chalet would be available to *L'Abri*. Chance? Oh, if you could only hear the intricate detail covering so many thousands of miles and so many years!

What couple came to take care of Les Sapins? It just "happened" that Debby—yes, our youngest daughter—and her husband Udo, had applied to be *L'Abri* Workers in Huémoz before we knew that Les Sapins was to be in *L'Abri*. Debby and Udo Middelmann were married four years ago in the twelfth-century Ollon church, where William Farel preached at the beginning of the Reformation. Memory carried us back through Priscilla's and Susan's weddings in the same building. The woodsy smells of fern, moss-covered logs and ivy filled the place as Jane Stuart Smith's voice once more thrilled us as it had when we first heard, "And Ruth said, thy people shall be my people, and thy God my God . . .", now years ago at Priscilla's wedding. As we looked around from the shining dark eyes of the bride as she came in on her father's arm to meet her tall blond groom, to the fascinated gaze of those watching her in the audience, we were struck by a continuity we never could have planned. There was a blending of the years among the guests, from early Lausanne days, our Champéry days, and *L'Abri*'s history, right up to the then present community. The continuity was that of a growing family, in two senses of the word. That wedding day we did not know what was coming four years later.

Debby taught French in John Burroughs school in St. Louis for three years while Udo went to theological school. Udo had graduated in law from Freiburg University in Germany just as Ranald had his law degree from Cambridge. Debby had graduated from the University of Lausanne, as Priscilla had. Just as Priscilla and John had considered many other possibilities of life-work so had Susan and Ranald, and later Debby and Udo. It is not because it is an "expected thing" or the "done thing" that our girls and their husbands (of three different nationalities) came back into the work of *L'Abri*. They believe it is God's choice for them, and year by year they and their husbands are seeing God's plan unfold for them in the work. To us it is a thing of wonder and awe to see how God has continued to make it a "family" shared, even as it was in the beginning, although the shared family now contains our "spiritual children" as well as our personal family.

Les Sapins had only been ours a few days before it was full, with thirty-five people sleeping in every available space, including the balconies. Had we not been given it at just that moment, thirty-five would have had to be turned away including about sixteen Africans.

Les Sapins has every available space full this year too, with guests, helpers and Farel House students, plus a new little Middelmann, Natasha, born to Debby and Udo on February 28th.

Five years ago Linette and Joe were still in the Bee man's house. Things have changed so much since then, as Linette and Joe bought a chalet at the other end of the village and named it "Bethany". Frances Kramer bought the Bee man's house— Bourdonette—and made the two apartments into one house. Bethany became the boys' dormitory and housed twenty-two people. Linette and Joe went to the States where Joe is finishing his degree. Their chalet is rented by *L'Abri* and, when Jeremy and Regina (the first wedding in the new chapel), who were the couple to care for it after Joe and Linette left, felt certain that they were needed in Ireland, it was Claire who took over the housekeeping, cooking and being hostess of Bethany. Others took over the carpentry shop which had been commenced by Jeremy in the garage at Bethany. Bob Holmes took Jeremy's place as host of Bethany as well as working on a card system for the discussion tapes. Each name suggests a story of course . . . but obviously each story can't be told. Claire, for instance, owned and ran her own beauty shop in southern California. What made her feel sure, after hearing the *L'Abri* Ensemble, that she should leave all this and her comfortable life and come to *L'Abri* willing to work hard with no financial return, would take a lot of space to tell. Also what made her fit into the work as though a clever personnel manager had screened her and picked her from applicants, would be impossible to tell.

As I have been trying to portray to you, we really have prayed, for thirteen years now, that God would send the Workers of His choice; and it has seemed clear to us that God has chosen a succession of people for the period of time He wanted them here . . . or He wants them here now. Os Guinness, for instance, not only sorts out the letters and keeps a complicated chart of how many people have already been promised beds, so that we can see how letters are to be answered to those asking for places, but he is also an excellent preacher and Bible expositor. Norma can not only do secretarial work but has had experience in typing manuscripts. Each Worker who has come and gone, or who continues to be here, we feel, has been brought by the Lord for a specific moment of history and a specific share in the work.

What has happened to Bourdonette? Mrs. Kramer has gone back to America to educate her children. Bourdonette has been rented by various families who wanted to be near *L'Abri* for a time.

In addition to the houses already mentioned, *L'Abri* rents a room in a village home for additional space, and rents a chalet—or house—squashed into the portion of the village where houses share common walls, named Rionzi. Rionzi was run by Claire for girls before she took over Bethany. Then it was used by a family coming to Farel House last winter. This summer the Rookmaakers are the *L'Abri* couple running Rionzi. Mrs. Rookmaaker is cooking and feeding people as well as having a six-bed bedroom full of girls, and a couple of small bedrooms. Professor Rookmaaker, in addition to giving lectures, is talking at meal times and with individuals who come to him for help. The Rookmaakers have been *L'Abri* Members for four years. The work in Holland has grown and has two other Workers, Hans van Seventer and his wife, JoAnn.

The work in Italy has also changed. The day came when Hurvey and Dorothy's apartment no longer needed to be used for church services, Sunday school and lecture or discussion evenings because a second apartment had been rented and furnished as a meeting place. Another addition was a permanent villa to be used for weekend conferences, summer and Easter camps and so forth, in San Fedele, a mountain village above Lake Como. Work in Italy is slow and discouraging but Hurvey and Dorothy have laid a fine foundation, and now a solid growth is coming, and the church, which is a congregation of our International Church (Presbyterian-Réformé), is growing. Hurvey is having openings in other areas, too, and is finding the same problem most of us have in being finite!

The chapel had been commenced when I wrote nearly five years ago, but it was not finished. The dedication day for the chapel came. Some months later the Flentrop organ was dedicated. Mr. and Mrs. Flentrop came from Holland for the dedication bringing with them a gift, Mr. Jansen to play for the service. He is a leading organist in Holland (organist of Amsterdam's West Church). Mr. Jansen gave a concert that golden October moonlit night, with Jane Stuart Smith singing her heart out with joy as answered prayer surrounded her with the organ's wonderful accompaniment. She had long prayed for an organ—and for this particular one, a hand-made baroque organ designed especially by the great Dutch organ maker for our little chalet chapel.

It was a kind of fairy-tale night. We listened to the marvellous tones of that organ, looking out at the breathtaking view of the Dents du Midi and the twinkling lights of the Rhône Valley below, all bathed in the yellow-white light of the moon, and afterwards walked back up to Chalet les Mélèzes for conversation and refreshments.

The chapel is full every Sunday now. All the chairs are full, and the extra floor space has people sitting on it on cushions. Benches have been placed on the balconies (they have to be carried back up to the chalets in time to serve dinner), and people sit on the outside steps leading down to Farel House. We are wondering what we can do about it. Church services, lectures, concerts, Saturday night discussions, and even Sunday night prayer meetings are crowded out these days. The organ and pulpit are up front, with the wall, which is all window, at one's left looking out over the fabulous view. But on the right, a third of the way from the back, is a large stone fireplace. For discussions, prayer meetings, communion services and some informal concerts, the fireplace is the "front" and people sit in a semi-circle facing the fire as it crackles and leaps up the chimney.

I mentioned the steps down to Farel House, so I must quickly go on to explain that the seven-desked Farel House in the sunroom held only fourteen students in two shifts, and, as you can imagine, that became too small. Under the new chapel was a long narrow strip of space—narrow because the chapel is on a sharp slope and one walks into it from ground level, though the balcony is hung out over space. That leaves a space which is a portion of the width though the same length as the chapel. We prayed for money to finish this off into a new Farel House, with perhaps a kitchen and toilets. The Lord sent the money by way of a legacy. My father's cousin, Marion Paden, was a missionary in Egypt for forty-five years. During these years she had taken summer vacations in Auliens, just down the hill half-way between Huémoz and Ollon. Bellevue, where the rehabilitation home is now, was a hotel in those days, as was the big square house down in Auliens. The missionaries used to walk up to have tea at Bellevue!

Cousin Marion's money, left to *L'Abri*, was to do two things. First, it finished off the new Farel House. It had enough space for sixteen desks with built-in tape-recorders. There was space left for a kitchen and two toilets. The kitchen, however, has now been made into additional Farel House space for more desks and tape-recorders. With two shifts, fifty can be cared for down there below the chapel, and sixteen in Beau Site, so capacity is sixty-six at present, with morning and afternoon shifts. We have had to make a new rule recently. Unless there is a strong reason for making an exception, Farel House students can only come for three months, as there are too many wanting to come for the available space.

Cousin Marion's money also bought a field, surrounded by a pine tree hedge—a lovely plot for building. At present the land is being used for growing beans, broccoli, peas and corn, as we continue to pray for the Lord's timing and also His plan for the use of the land. Again, it is easy to think one knows the next step before it is made absolutely clear.

I have mentioned tapes and tape-recorders. One day, some years ago, a businessman was taking an early morning plane ride from one city in the States to another. He was reading a *L'Abri* Family Letter which a cousin had passed on to him to look at. As he read, so he told us in a letter, he felt strongly compelled to send us a tape-recorder, really having no idea what we might do with it; thinking perhaps he ought to send some taped sermons along with it. When that tape-recorder arrived Fran made some very dogmatic statements. He would never stick a microphone up in front of him; that would squash out all spontaneity, questions would cease to flow, the reality of what was happening would be spoiled. "Leave it in its box . . . no use even opening it."

And so it sat for six months in the huge cardboard box in the office. One night John Boice (an early Worker at *L'Abri*, now a missionary in South America) was listening to the very rapid succession of questions which were coming from a group of Smith College girls, and the answers being given. "Brilliant," he thought to himself, "and following such a logical sequence. Wish it could be recorded."

It was a Saturday night; I was finishing the dishwashing and making ice-cream for Sunday dinner, when John stuck his head in the kitchen. "Could you serve tea to the people in the discussion? I have an idea, and I need a little clatter to accomplish it." Soon a tray was ready with cups and saucers, milk, sugar, a steaming pot of tea and a bowlful of freshly popped corn. Serving made a clatter and brought forth chatter, which distracted attention while John successfully hid a microphone in some plants growing in the bookcase with its copper plant holder. When the discussion, questions and answers were resumed, everything was being recorded! The results were produced by John the next day, and as the girls listened to their questions and the answers for a second time, their reaction was one of delight.

"Oh, great, I was so afraid I'd forget what he said, and I do want one of my friends to hear this too . . . please could I buy a copy?" This was echoed by each one of them. So the first tape was made and immediately used.

Farel House began with individual study for four hours each morning, the reading of papers prepared in these hours, discussions of such papers in seminars, and personal discussions with Fran as Senior Tutor. However, as the first year slipped into the second year, Fran began what he called "Farel House Luncheons". I was to serve lunch silently, and during the three courses of food he gave lectures. The first series was called "The Intellectual Climate of the New Theology". Because a few new students were expected, and because it would be impossible to go over the first lectures in order to have them understand the middle ones, someone said, "Let's put the tape-recorder on the radiator in the dining-room, and fix the microphone near Dr. Schaeffer's place . . . right there above his knife." And so the first lecture tape was made! It is still being listened to, with the noise of forks and clinking of spoons against cups!

As the English trips continued and Fran had discussions in the private rooms of men in Cambridge, Oxford, St. Andrews, Glasgow, and so on, various men produced their own tape-recorders, and hence many of these discussions were preserved, some of them absolutely unrepeatable—such as the time when twenty atheists were firing questions during an evening in Cambridge. This can still be heard.

As time went on the tapes were so much in demand and such a help in Huémoz, that all Saturday nights began to be recorded, plus sermons on Sunday, and doctrinal teaching in the Bible classes in Harro and Ann's apartment in Lausanne.

As Farel House grew, two things happened. Rather than the Farel House luncheons, it became necessary to have lectures in the evenings, undisturbed by eating, so that students could take notes. These lectures have all been preserved on tape, and have been formed into a tape library which was begun by Richard Ducker. At present there are more than 850 hours of tapes, catalogued into subject matter. For years now the Farel House students have selected, with Dr. Schaeffer as Senior Tutor advising them individually, the subjects they wish to hear, and have followed courses on tape. They listen with earphones and the desks are equipped with individual tape-recorders. As we pray still for the help that is needed we include prayer for electrical engineers who can repair tape-recorders —a constant problem! The story of the various personalities who have been sent to repair the tape-recorders would make a very long chapter.

Tapes have also been copied and sent out to those wanting to hear them elsewhere. At first, Jeremy Jackson, a Worker for a year or so, copied tapes. Then, as John Sandri came into the work, he took over two large parts of it: as Treasurer of *L'Abri*, and as the one who copies tapes, packages them up and sends them off to many corners of the earth. He has made "tape lists" so that people may see the scope of subject matter, and order the lectures which interest them.

Without advertising, the "tape work" of *L'Abri* (if that is a good way of speaking of it) has grown beyond our imagination. Tapes are listened to by individuals, and also by groups. Tape listening sessions are taking place in widely scattered parts of the world: Taiwan, Japan, India, South Africa, France, South America, Switzerland, Canada, New Zealand, Australia, England, Scotland, Ireland, Germany, Holland and in so many scattered states . . . California, Virginia, Illinois, Pennsylvania, Massachusetts and so on. We really haven't any idea ourselves of the scope. People continually come to *L'Abri* saying, "Oh, I heard a tape in such and such a place. . . ."— when we have never heard of such a tape-listening group ourselves. Could we have planned this if we had tried to?

Then came the day when a businessman in the States, Bill Wysor, who felt his income was adequate to live on and that he would like to give his life to God's work, offered to make his home a centre for tapes. He said he would stock tapes and have a lending library in his home in Virginia, and would himself do the tedious work of packaging them, sending them off, repairing torn tapes as they arrived back and send them off again. Not a glamorous work, nor a naturally attractive work to a man who has had a whole company of men to work for him before. This man happens to be a cousin of Jane Stuart Smith and he first heard Fran when he spoke at Jane's father's funeral. It was then that he began considering the possibility of all this being truth. He had been a Christian for a number of years before he actually came to *L'Abri* for a summer, renting Bourdonette and living in the midst of the community with his family.

What is being said in these tapes? What are the answers being given? Why has *L'Abri* become known as a "Mission to intellectuals" (not our label, but one given by *Time* magazine in an article)? Some of the answers to some of the questions are recorded in two books currently on sale in England and

America, and soon to be in other languges. *Escape from Reason* and *The God Who is There* were both written because a series of lectures (one in England; one in America) were taped, typed and thrust into my husband's hands to work up into a book. You may conclude what you like, of course, but we felt it was God's unfolding of a new portion of His plan in answer to our prayer, as we turned our lives to the possibility of His being able to communicate it through us.

Udo has, as his portion of the work, the area of publishing as well as being Junior Tutor of Farel House. Other lectures are coming forth and other books and booklets. Not only is Professor Rookmaaker writing on art and jazz (two areas in which he is an expert) but the other *L'Abri* Members and Workers are writing too. We have no idea what is ahead in publishing, but books and booklets are already out and not only are Workers writing, but young creative poets, writers and artists are preparing to express what they feel will communicate truth to the twentieth-century generation. Young Christians at *L'Abri* are planning to produce a film which they feel will communicate Christianity as truth; an actor at *L'Abri* at present is planning television productions; a landscape architect, a sculptor, a photographer, an educator are excited about ideas. In other words, a whole flood of creativity is being released as if a dam had been removed, and we can only guess at the possibilities ahead.

There are those who have become Christians, not through a leap of faith on the basis of emotionalism, but on the basis of certainty in the area of logical answers to the real questions which are at the root of the too-often surface considerations. Then, on the basis of making a choice in a given moment of history, they have submitted to the God who is there. They have a burning desire to communicate the truth of the universe and the existence of God in the medium of their own talents.

"Surely you have the usual overhead expenses, a 'home office' in America with secretaries, a paid treasurer and so forth? It must have had to go into the usual channels in these areas?"

The amazing thing to us is that it has not. It is still a "family" sharing work. Karl and Alida Woodson took over the work of receiving and transmitting gifts and sending out news letters, at the time of Mother's death, when Father felt he could not go on doing all this alone. Karl teaches instrumental music and leads the orchestra in a Detroit high school. Alida is mother of four small children.

They give evenings and weekends to doing *L'Abri* work. They feel as much a part of *L'Abri* as when they worked in Huémoz, in spite of missing the advantages of actually meeting the people as they come and go.

The community in Huémoz is to have another addition this autumn, too. A chapter must be condensed into a paragraph to tell you about it. It is to us the answer to many prayers. We have long prayed for a school on the level of university preparation, which would integrate the teaching and show the relationships between a wide number of subjects, in a framework similar to that which *L'Abri* has in its discussions, relating philosophy to history, art and music, and showing the relationship of various disciplines to Christianity. We did not pray that such a school would necessarily be in our midst but we prayed for the existence of such a school.

Peter Farrow, an English graduate of Keele University, who taught in an international school in Switzerland and then became Headmaster of another one for a period of time, had also been praying about a school which he hoped to commence to prepare for the International Baccalaureate, for English-speaking young people in Switzerland. The story of how God brought us together, how suddenly the square, white house in Auliens (fifteen minutes' walk down the hill), with its 3,500 square metres of land, came up for rent with an option to buy; of how the owner remembers Cousin Marion teaching his wife English as she stayed in it during its hotel days in the 1930's, is a long and wonderful one. Suffice it to say that it seems another fantastic pattern of threads which have been woven for years. This white house is to become the *Ecole du Monde* this autumn, separate organisationally from *L'Abri*, but part of the community. *L'Abri* people will lead the students in the same kind of seminars we use with Farel house students and guests. Who can say what is ahead, as twelve- to eighteen-year-old young people become a part of the community, and have this place as a part of their background to life.

Jumping from one change to another, from one big answer to prayer to another, from one surprise development to another may give a false impression. I have found this a nerve-racking chapter to write. It has not been an exciting succession of "success". There have been sicknesses, accidents, depressions, discouragement, frustrations and exhaustion. There has been a succession of difficulties which arise from having little money, a succession of temptations to give up, to call it too much, to say we have had enough and that we want to have a "normal life like other people". There have been what we feel sure are direct attacks of Satan to stop us, to make us give up. If you want to read what the Bible says about living by "faith", read in Hebrews the 11th chapter, and the first four verses of the 12th. It is not an account of easy lives and a succession of "high points". To say the least, there is a variety of things to be experienced. It is far from a soft life.

But there is *reality*. There is certainty of the God who is there. There is the possibility of seeing that God works in space, time and history, and in one's own moment of history. There is the certainty of being in communication with Him rather than having some nebulous psychological crutch to enable one to bear life!

I want to say something before finishing on what God has done in the past thirteen years in developing and training a man in His own way, as well as in developing a work. "Where did your husband get all this?" "At what universities did he study to get this which he is giving?" "Where can we buy the books he has read to prepare this stuff?" "Your husband has a new apologetic, that is such an influence . . . you have no idea how it is changing man's approach . . . but *where* did he get it?"

It would be a short cut for me to say that "God gave it to him", as it can be told in a more understandable fashion. We prayed for the ones of God's choice to be sent to us. We believe the people who have come, have come for help they themselves needed. However, we believe God can do two things at once. (A masterpiece of understatement!) In this case I am certain He brought people for their own sakes but also brought a variety of people as a training-ground and as a means of developing, in the arena of live conversation, that which Fran is giving in his apologetic today. Rather than studying volumes in an ivory tower separated from life, and developing a theory separated from the thinking and struggling of men, Fran has been talking for thirteen years now to men and women in the very midst of their struggles. He has talked to existentialists, logical positivists, Hindus, Buddhists, liberal Protestants, liberal Roman Catholics, Reformed Jews and atheistic Jews, Muslims, members of occult cults and people of a wide variety of religions and philosophies, as well as atheists of a variety of types. He has talked to brilliant professors, brilliant students and brilliant drop-outs! He has talked to beatniks, hippies, drug addicts, homosexuals and psychologically disturbed people. He has talked to Africans, Indians, Chinese, Koreans, Japanese, South Americans, people from the islands of the sea, from Australia and New Zealand and from all the European countries as well as from America and Canada. He has talked to people of many different political colours. He has talked to doctors, lawyers, scientists, artists, writers, engineers, research men in many fields, philosophers, businessmen, newspapermen and actors, famous people and peasants. He has talked to both generations! In it all God has been giving him an education which it is not possible for many people to have. The answers have been given, not out of academic research (although he does volumes of reading constantly to keep up) but out of this arena of live conversation. He answers real questions with carefully thought out answers which are the real answers. He gets excited himself as he comes to me often saying, "It really *is* the answer, Edith; it fits, it really fits. It really *is* truth, and because it is true it fits what is really there." The excitement is genuine. This is what I mean when I say God has given him an education in addition to unfolding a work in these past thirteen years.

Have I finished? There is more to be covered to show you what God has done. A family of six, two of them sick children, move into a beaten up chalet in a tiny mountain village without even a living-room . . . and pray that God will send them the people to talk to! They "bury" themselves as far as this world's

227

standards go, and should never be heard of again. And as they pray, the people come; the room is finally packed with fifty; doors are taken off and sixty are included within earshot; the chapel holds over 150 now and then some on balconies and steps. God has pushed out the walls in a very real way. Another way He has had of "pushing out the wall" to allow more people to listen has been in the Italian, English and Dutch trips, and then, in the last three years, the American trips. In accepting speaking engagements and giving a series of lectures, far more invitations have been refused from all over the world. The accepted ones have taken us, in the United States, from Boston to San Francisco, from Chicago to Tennessee, from St. Louis to Seattle. Colleges, seminaries, gatherings of a variety of people: Harvard, Massachusetts Institute of Technology, Wellesley, Stanford, Berkeley, Wheaton, Westmont, Covenant . . . a variety of places and types have been brought into earshot of that Swiss fireside conversation. Last January, in one three-day period Fran took part in a dialogue with Bishop Pike in a Chicago auditorium on a bitterly cold night in the midst of a blizzard. Over 2,500 people were there, and, because of two television programmes and three radio programmes on which Fran was asked to discuss and answer questions, the walls of the Mélèzes' living-room suddenly flattened out and 3,000,000 people came in for a short period to hear the conversation during those three days.

I would like to finish by quoting from an Israelite who wrote many years ago: "O Lord God, thou hast begun to show thy servant thy greatness, and thy mighty hand: for what God is there in heaven or in earth, that can do according to thy works, and according to thy might?" (Deuteronomy 3:24). And again from another: "Then ye shall let your children know, saying, Israel came over this Jordan on dry land. For the Lord your God dried up the waters of Jordan from before you, until you were passed over, as the Lord your God did to the Red Sea, which he dried up from before us, until we were gone over: that all the people of the earth might know the hand of the Lord, that it is mighty: that ye might fear the Lord your God for ever" (Joshua 4:22–4).